MOVE CLOSER STAY LONGER

Dr. Stephanie Burns

Don't let fear keep you from getting what you want, doing what you want, and going where you want to go.

Published by Navybridge Pty Ltd

Copyright Stephanie Burns 1993-2010

This work is copyright. Apart from fair dealing for the purposes of scholarship or review, and subject to the Copyright Act 1968, no part of this publication may be reproduced, stored in a retrieval system, or transmitted in any form, or by any means, electronic, mechanical, photocopying, recording, or otherwise, without the prior written permission of the publisher.

Produced in Australia by Navybridge Pty Limited
P.O. Box 53
North Sydney, NSW 2069

Burns, Stephanie
Move Closer Stay Longer
ISBN 9781450534888
1. Learning.
2. Learning, Psychology of.
3. Study, Method of.
I. Title

Other written works by the author

The Emotional Experience of the Adult Learner

Artistry In Training

Great Lies We Live By

Photography by
Coco/Firefly Fotos & Helen Hall

To Linda and Pat Parelli
Helen Hall
Nugget and Buddy

The true stars of the story

CONTENTS

Foreword by Stephanie Burns   3

Being Afraid
This is a Story About Fear   7
The Nature of Fear   12
Transformations of Fear   30
Just What is Bravery?   43
Reality Test   48

The Bravery Strategy
Move Closer Stay Longer   63
Common Mistakes   69

Action
Don't Think, Just Do It   82
Do Think   88
Just Start, Decide Later   93
Measure and Count   97
Challenge Your Assumptions with Quality Information   102
Use the Power of Commitments to Other People as Motivation   108
Do Lots of What You Can Do and a Little of What You Are Afraid Of   111

Time
Time Will Pass   94

Acknowledgements   119

FOREWORD

by Stephanie Burns

When I was asked to write a book about fear I wondered how I would approach such a difficult and personal topic. In my own life I know how crafty I can be at creating excuses to avoid people, places, objects, situations and tasks that frighten me. I knew that simple positive aspirations and corny lines made me go deeper into avoidance. I didn't want to write a corny book. I wanted to tell the truth through my own story.

We are fragile in relation to achieving goals when fear is involved. It is not about FEELING THE FEAR AND DOING IT ANYWAY. It is not about the kind of courage John Wayne spoke of when he said, "Courage is being scared to death and saddling up anyway." I would not, and most of you would not even take a first step if that were the only strategy available. What it IS about is having an understanding of our behavior and working with it to our best benefit.

What I want you to learn is that fear is not the problem. It is responsible for our safety and ultimately our survival. Do we really need to wonder why we so consistently avoid activities that cross its path? It is not only fear that causes avoidance either. It could be boredom, apathy, or confusion. Not knowing that fear or some other negative emotion is NOT THE PROBLEM causes us to put our effort in the wrong place.

The problem is an inability or lack of willingness to take action. There is no change or learning if you cannot motivate yourself to act. Life is long and how much you create within its boundaries has everything to do with both the mental and physical actions you take.

The combination of the bravery strategy of *MOVE CLOSER, STAY LONGER* and the motivation strategies I present in this book will enable you to interrupt the mechanisms that fear uses to interfere with the actions you want to take. How they do this is by helping you control what you do and not do and what you think about and what you do not think about.

Even so, there will be times when fear interferes with your ability to use these cognitive tools. When I observed this happen in my experience with my horse, Nugget, I knew that I had to find something more to enable me to stay in the game. I did not want to give up but I hit such big barriers I could not get myself out there. The motivation strategies I will describe to you in the final chapters are exactly those that came to the forefront and kept me moving. To have not included them here would have been to let many of you down.

I am a teacher by choice. Therefore, this book like all my other written works is an attempt to teach. It matters to me that people have what they need to get wherever it is they think they want to go. I believe having constructed this conceptualization of bravery as a strategy may help some of you when fear is the cause for a potential failure.

My last day with Buddy before flying home from the Pat Parelli Center in Colorado to Australia

One thing is a certainty: Time will pass whether you do anything to achieve your goals or not. You can wake up in ten years and play the guitar or not. You can wake up having written a book or not. Time does not care where you go, what you do or what you achieve. The better part of your brain does not care either. Your brain only cares that you feel good and survive. The part of your brain that you use to dream about goals, well, that part does care. You should care. And, you should have every opportunity to get what you want, do what you want to do and go where you want to go.

I hope what you find on these pages is a part of what creates your opportunity. Go well.

Stephanie Burns

Being Afraid

*You cannot rightly be called
a wimp when you avoid
or delay activities that
scare you.*

CHAPTER 1

This is a Story About Fear

This is a true story of my adventures learning how to play with and ride horses. It was not my idea to have this adventure but one I FELL INTO. It is an important story not because I learned to ride a horse but because of what I had to do to accomplish that goal. This is a story about fear.

I have spent the majority of my career working, in one way or another, in the service of helping people get where it is they say they want to go. I study and am fascinated by human behaviour. I have been successful in the development of various strategies to help people navigate life pursuits and achieve personal goals.

Along the way, the study of emotions, and the effect they

have on learning and achievement became an important part of my work. In fact, it was the focus of my PhD research. But at no time had it been necessary for me to focus exclusively on "fear".

Not, that is, until I met horseman Pat Parelli and his wife Linda.

Pat Parelli is a phenomenon in the horse world. He and those in his organization are changing the way people teach horses and horses teach people. The Queen of England, after watching Pat work one of her difficult horses in a demonstration, said she only wished she'd met Pat much earlier. The FFE (French Federation Equitation) in France requires all of their instructors to be qualified to teach the Seven Games and basis of horse psychology defined by Pat's program. Olympians such as Gold Medalist David O'Connor and his wife Karen endorse and use Pat Parelli's method to ensure that those involved competitively and professionally with horses understand the importance of his contribution. His work is informed and respected by many of the world's best horseman present and past.

Linda is Pat's Australian wife. She has a long history with horses and is a masterful teacher. She is responsible for bringing Pat's work to the many people who seek it by writing much of what has been written about Pat and his methods. I met Linda many years ago when she was a student in several of my courses. Unbeknownst to me she took concepts from those courses to use in the development of the lessons taught to students and *Parelli* instructors. An invisible thread connected us from that time forward. Today that thread of connection is strong and very visible.

It was through Linda's tenacity that Pat and I finally sat around the same table. The rest as they say IS HISTORY.

As part of my work I am often required to personally reenter the world of the adult learner. By taking what I know about learning and achievement and then walking a mile in the moccasins of the learner allows me to create two things: a good understanding of that particular learning process, and a set of strategies to support the learner. My research into the nature of fear in the context of learning and achievement came about as the result of *THE PARELLI PROJECT*.

I was asked by Pat and Linda to create a set of learning and motivational strategies to support students of the *Parelli Natural Horse•Man•Ship Savvy System* home school program. Many thousands of students use the Savvy System program as the only means by which they can study with Pat. My job was to create a learning support website where remote students could go for support if, and when, they ran into learning and motivation barriers.

I had a bag full of learning and motivation strategies that could be used to support people in many kinds of goals that required learning. But after reviewing the home study materials in preparation for my writing, I discovered that the process for the *Parelli* student was very dynamic. Support for students in Pat's program would require significantly more sensitivity and creativity than, say, support for someone who is learning to juggle or learning to improve reading skills.

To do justice to the project I needed to experience being a *Parelli* student first hand. There have been adults with little previous experience with horses who do the *Parelli* program successfully. I felt confident that I, too, could achieve Level 1 in the program. That meant that I would learn to safely play with and ride a horse. I felt that after achieving this myself I could more legitimately create learning and motivation strategies that not only would work but also would make sense to a *Parelli* student.

Before I could start there were a few problems to overcome. Simple things like I didn't have a horse. Actually I had never touched a horse. And a few complicated things like I lived on a 1/12th-acre property on Sydney's Middle Harbour, enjoying the city life.

It took a little over a year to get myself organised. I sold up in the city and bought a property on 5 acres outside of Sydney. I went to a *Parelli* event to get a bit closer to horses. I touched a horse on the nose, and then on the neck and back for the first time ever. I was prepared by *Parelli* instructors to care for and to safely be in close proximity to the big, powerful animal that a horse is. I declined work contracts that required I travel so I could be home with my first ever horse. His name is Nugget and he is central to this story.

With all this done I was ready to experience the process of being a Level 1 student in the *Parelli Natural Horse•Man•Ship Savvy System* home study program.

There was one small problem.

After all that preparation for the project, reading books, watching videos, spending time studying basic horse handling with instructors, I learned to have a whopping big fear of horses, including my dear fellow Nugget.

If I had not grown to care so much for what Pat and Linda were trying to do for horses and the people who own them I don't believe I would have or could have persisted. But because of it I was determined to keep my commitment. To do that I used every morsel of knowledge about human behaviour, and every strategy for learning and motivation I possessed to enable me to be a legitimate student.

Of course, my learning process was heavily littered with barriers caused by my fear. Because of this experience I created very well defined concepts about the nature of fear in learning and achievement. I also created viable bravery strategy that I could use to take action toward this goal even at the scariest times.

Two things resulted from this experience. First, I was able to take the actions necessary to achieve Level 1 in Pat's program and continue on in the program as I do today.

By using what I knew about myself as the student, I was able to create a fundamental change in my fear response to horses. Now, I play with and ride horses with confidence and because I WANT TO.

This is a book about fear and therefore the stories are of conflict and challenge, but it should never be thought that there were more shrieks than laughs. That just wouldn't be true. The *Parelli* program is outstanding at moving people and horses from where they are to somewhere better. For this book I simply had to focus on the rocks on the road.

Lastly, I would like you to know that this is NOT a book about horses nor was it written particularly for horse lovers. My experiences that I tell as stories in this book help me to help you understand the points I would like you to learn. The content of this book is about the nature of fear, and the development of bravery such that you, too, can persist when something you have to do, to get where you want to go, causes you to be afraid and avoid action.

For the horse lovers and *Parelli* students who do read this book, enjoy the mile you will now walk in my shoes. Perhaps you will relate to some of the challenges I stared squarely in the face and figured out how to jump over.

My hope for all readers is that you can be brave enough to take action, stay long enough to feel a change so that you may one day forget that you were ever afraid.

— Stephanie Burns, Sydney, 2004

CHAPTER 2

The Nature of Fear

For me to undertake the adventure of being a *Parelli* student so I could help other students meant that first a horse had to be found that could come and live with me. I knew enough to know that I did not have enough experience to choose my own horse. The only qualities I could tease out of meeting a horse for the first time were its colour and size and I had been taught that these were not the qualities that mattered most, if at all when choosing a horse. I listened to everything said about finding the right horse.

Finding a horse for me caused MUCHO fear in other people. It was turning out that there were people with a lot of advice but no solution. No one really wanted to be responsible for killing or otherwise maiming Pat and Linda Parelli's good friend. That would cause them to lose face.

During the months I did not have my own horse I went to a place where I played with someone else's horse that was not SUITABLE for me to buy because he was not a CONFIDENT horse. He was red and his name was Cooper. It made me sad and confused because he was suitable for me to play with and ride on but not for me to bring home and feed. None of my experiences with Cooper ever caused me to feel fear.

Having not had any personal experiences that would have instilled a fear of horses when I started this adventure causes me to think that a lot of my fears started as I listened to the long list of all the possible dangers in having the wrong horse. I was told that Cooper was the WRONG HORSE. These stories taught me to be afraid of Cooper and I found myself making less frequent trips to play with him.

It took two good and cautious friends, Owen and Kate Gwinn, now retired *Parelli* instructors to suggest that they might have found a SUITABLE horse. What I remember most about the description of this horse was that he was PLAIN (just brown and short). I was told, "He couldn't jump or buck worth a damn," and he had passed all his basic horse-anality tests. His name was Nugget and I thought Nugget was a cute name until Pat said that everyone in Australia has a horse named Nugget. He was 4 years old.

To be on the safe side and KEEPING THE DOOR OPEN about being wrong about Nugget it was suggested that a good idea for an introduction and TRIAL RUN would be to play with Nugget in a Level 1 clinic with other *Parelli* students for 1 week. In that way I could see if Nugget was suitable. This was a good idea.

Being he might be a WRONG HORSE I was too nervous to go myself. I sent my long time friend and partner on this project Helen.

Fear is important. Most of you would know fear as one type of emotion that is experienced by humans and animals alike. But what you may or may not know is that every emotion has a specific purpose. In the big scheme fear is about survival. In the more mundane scheme it is about protecting you from loss.

Your brain has as its primary mission to keep you alive and in GOOD SHAPE long enough to reproduce. To this end, emotions, like fear, are essential. Emotions come as a standard feature in all humans and animals.

The purpose of fear is to protect you from loss

*Loss of resources (money, friends, things),
loss of love
loss of self-esteem
and most importantly, loss of life.*

Fear keeps you safe and out of harms way

It is also paradoxical. Having a fear of horses did protect me from losing limbs and life in the presence of one, and my friends from losing face for having given me the one that did it to me. But that same fear just as easily undermined my desired goal of having the experience with horses I was seeking to have. Fear is very tricky.

It can and does cause us to fail to achieve the very goals we are striving toward. Because fear is about more than just the loss of life it gets in the way of many different kinds of goals. Fear prevents some people from asking for a deserved raise, seeing a doctor, asking for directions when they are lost, giving a speech, or asking someone to go on a date. Understanding the nature of fear can help you to keep fear intact for the good it does, but override it when it unnecessarily gets in your way.

As emotions go, fear is well understood. It is studied more than any other emotion. People write songs about love, but they write books, and lots of them, about fear.

How do emotions, like fear, fulfil their purposes?

Each emotion is a unique program that your brain executes to quickly get the rest of your body and mind ready to do something specific. Emotions are called ACTION-READINESS PROGRAMS. As the name implies, it is a program to prepare your body for an appropriate response. Your whole body and everything in it is involved with an action-readiness program.

The action-readiness program caused by fear is to run, duck and dodge if you can, to turn and fight if you are trapped, and to avoid doing things that scare you when you can get away with it.

Speaking of which, I cheerily sent Helen off each morning to the clinic with Nugget. When she expressed concerns or anxiety about what she had done or was to do the next day I supported and encouraged her. I am good at that. There is nothing wrong with my action-readiness program for fear!

The night before the last day of the clinic Helen was not in very good emotional shape. She was what is called an EMOTIONAL MESS. So far Nugget had been a good horse. He was a confident horse, played well on the ground and was calm when ridden. He hadn't bucked even once. When he got a fright he took a small jump and looked at whatever caused it. He never showed any propensity for running off with her attached. He was clever at going to a tree just not the one Helen was trying to get to. He had faulty steering.

Helen was a mess because she could not determine if he should come to live with me the next day or be sent back. She was running the action-readiness program for sadness. She did not know how to make an intelligent decision but now IT WAS CRUNCH TIME and she was crying so I just made one. I decided Nugget would come home for some more TRIALLING, and Helen stopped crying.

I was much too afraid to drive him home myself. So I made arrangements for Nugget to be brought home by a HORSE COMPETENT friend on the weekend.

How does an action-readiness program work?

It is easiest to answer this question with a couple of examples. Let's say I am walking down a country lane and my eye picks up a pattern that is familiar. My attention is drawn to that pattern and a part of my brain asks, "What is that?" Let's say it determines that the pattern has a name "horse".

It then asks, "What does 'horse' mean?"

Depending on lots of things in my past the answer might be that 'horse' means fun and excitement. If so, my brain will begin to run the action-readiness program for excitement. That program causes my heart rate to increase, my eyes to focus on the pattern and my voice to activate. I call out "Hey" to get the horse's attention as I run to it to say, "Hello".

But what if the only thing I know about horses are the scary stories I have heard about being bitten and kicked and bucked off of horses seemingly without any reason. My brain might calculate that the 'horse' pattern means something very different. Like FEAR FOR MY LIFE because I don't know what a horse will do to me. Then, my brain will start a different action-readiness program. The one for fear that causes me to avert my eyes, to turn away quickly and walk swiftly in the other direction.

Emotions start in your brain as a calculation and then they get the rest of your body involved. **Your heart** rate changes to push more or less blood through your system. **Your skin** might flush with increased blood flow like when you blush or when your ears get hot. It might tingle, or get moist from sweat. **Your muscles** can change tension and cause you to clench your fists, or scrunch up your brow, or shrug your shoulders. **Your stomach** juices get active which can cause you to have "butterflies" or feel nauseous. **Your hair** can stand up to make you look larger to an approaching enemy (although this is more effective if you are a dog). **Movement ticks** kick in and can cause you to start rubbing, tapping, scratching, picking or biting things on yourself. And, unbidden **vocal bursts** can spew forth and you will say things like 'Oh no', 'Arghhh', 'Owww', or any number of expletives!

I experienced the action-readiness program of excitement for the entire night before Nugget arrived home and for as long as it took for him to step off the horse trailer. Then, without any warning, fear kicked in and all the above bodily effects that correspond with fear's action-readiness program took over. I mustered enough courage and courtesy to walk up to Nugget for a quick horse-handshake by stretching the back of my hand toward his nostril so he could smell me like he would if I was another horse. Fortunately, Helen was there. She walked him to the paddock while I went to the house to get a beer. I spent my first day of horse partnership watching this big beautiful animal (no longer plain, brown and short) from the safety of the porch.

> *The action-readiness program triggered by an emotion affects behaviour!*

Fear is always about something

A fear response is never about nothing. It will be about an object, a place, a person, a situation, or a task. Even if you cannot identify what is scaring you or causing you to be nervous it will never be nothing. It will always be something.

The thing that causes your fear response could be "out there" in your environment, such as, a loud cracking noise in the dead of night, a rustling sound in tall grass or the sight of your boss.

The thing that causes your fear response could just as well be nothing at all in reality but instead it could be something you are thinking about. Sometimes you cause this response by dwelling on a future event such as an upcoming test. Sometimes it seems to happen outside of your control, such as, being woken in the night with an unbidden thought about a dog running out from behind a bush while you are jogging.

Now remember, at this point in the story I had only had good experiences playing with and riding Cooper (I use the term 'riding' very loosely). I had only had stories and evidence of Nugget's good and calm nature.

I didn't allow myself to have many experiences with Nugget for the first few weeks he lived with me. I was having the worst kind of fear. I was afraid of being afraid so my fear program was working overtime figuring out ways to get Helen to do everything. She brushed him and washed his tail and picked out his hooves. When she did this I hid in my office. The fear response caused by simply watching this was too much for me and I was afraid for her. Of course, that didn't stop me from encouraging her.

I stacked on the praise and acknowledgement when she suggested riding Nugget in the paddock. I couldn't come outside to watch so I made sure she had a walkie-talkie with her to call for help if she ran into strife and then prayed that I would never hear her voice coming out of the little speaker. She just had to be brave first if I was ever going to get into this thing with Nugget. I adored him but could not bring myself to get near him.

Helen's first ride on Nugget in the paddock

Everything that was driving my behaviour was happening in my crazy mind thinking about the things I would have to do later when the pressures of the *Parelli* project came to weigh down on me.

The action-readiness program for fear works in two ways depending upon whether the fear is about something happening right NOW or if it is being triggered about something you are going to do sometime in the future. I needed strategies to cope with the latter situations right away, and the RIGHT NOW ones wouldn't be far behind. You will too, so now is a good point to learn the basic concepts.

Fear NOW!

If the fear response is about something that is happening right NOW in real time then the action-readiness program will get your body fully prepared and ready to RUN! HIDE! DUCK! FAINT! Whatever is that will best protect you at that time. It not only gets your body and mind prepared it actually starts the program running.

You do not have to do anything to consciously help yourself. If you have ever watched a movie where in one instant the music blares and the scene changes to one that is frightening, you will have experienced this action-readiness program kick in. You will either be on your neighbour's lap or half way up the aisle before the rest of your brain can calculate there is nothing real to fear. It can then take a while for the rest of your body, now fully charged, to calm down after your brain has given you the all clear. You may feel your heart beating inside your chest long afterward.

We share this use of our fear action-readiness program with all animals. I have a parrot named Kelly. For some reason I never developed fears about him so I play with him a lot.

A sudden loud bang will start a fear program that causes him to fly flat out to my shoulder. That is his flight response. He will slam right into the side of my head for safety. He will be securely hunkered into my neck long before the rest of his little birdbrain realises it was a book that fell from the shelf next to his perch and not the sky falling. He flees to safety first, and thinks rationally later. Better to be safe than dead.

Nugget has this program too. He, like Kelly, is a prey animal and his fear program is also dominantly geared toward flight. I often thought that it was a good thing horses can not fly.

When your brain calculates that you are in harms way you cannot turn off the response (nor would you want to). On the days when there is indeed a bear behind the tree, it is this brain function that will save your life if it is to be saved at all.

Anticipated fear

The second thing that can cause the action-readiness program for fear to run is when you ANTICIPATE a FEAR NOW experience in the future. This is something only humans do. Kelly, the parrot, does not sit on his perch worrying about whether today will be the day he will fall off while asleep even though he does occasionally fall off his perch and scare the bejeepers out of himself. He just does not use that experience to calculate a possible future experience.

But your very human brain has the ability to calculate that something you are thinking about doing in the future has a possible harmful consequence. Now, an action-readiness program that gets you to hide in the closet 3 days before your public presentation is not useful. ANTICIPATED FEAR RESPONSES cause your brain to start scheming. It starts working to figure out a way to get you to NOT do it!

That is a tricky job for a few pounds of brain!

Is fear good or bad?

As the weeks passed I began to experience an interesting emotional change. I was starting to experience a DESIRE to be the one doing some things with Nugget. I did not have any good stories stacking up about my time with horses. How could I ever have a FEAR NOW experience, let alone a FUN NOW experience, if I could not get out of my head and onto the horse?

I was still watching videos of Pat and listening to Helen telling me stories about her time with Nugget and I REALLY wanted to participate.

I had no evidence from my time watching Helen that I would in fact be killed or harmed. What had started out as such an exciting adventure was being lost in the muck of my mind.

I was also beginning to feel like a fraud. Here I was meant to be a *Parelli* home study student so I could use what I know about learning and motivation to help others. And for no good reason I could name I was doing nothing.

The PROVERBIAL WORM WAS ABOUT TO TURN. Things were about to change.

Without question fear is good in the general sense. It has saved your life and other resources on many occasions already this lifetime. But in specific cases, maybe it is good and maybe it isn't.

Let me use a common example and ask, "Is a fear of taking tests, which you need to do to complete a study program good, or bad?"

The answer is "It depends."

It depends on how the action-readiness program for fear is applied? If the program causes you to study more vigilantly it is very good to have a fear of taking tests. If the program causes you to drop out of the course then I would say that having a fear of taking a test is not a good thing for you.

Fear can be good if it causes you to behave cautiously and to be diligent in your preparations or if it causes you to be vigilant, to pay attention to detail and to be disciplined.

Reflecting on this was the breakthrough I needed. It caused many things to change within me. I had not remembered that I get paid to help people through similar experiences. All along I had been helping Helen, who had a REAL fear of horses when all this started, to get out there to participate and learn from which she was gaining more and more confidence. I KNEW that my fear of Nugget stepping on my toe could cause me to take the extra effort to ensure I had proper shoes on just as much as it might cause me to avoid being near him. It was time I started to coach myself.

Later this day I picked up the first Pocket Guide in my *Parelli Level 1 Partnership* program and went out to be with Nugget. It was a great experience too because as I sat out in Nugget's paddock in the sun reading he came over to read over my shoulder. Then he lay down next to me.

I sent Linda an email and told her about this story and sent her the photos. She emailed back one line, "That's not normal!!" In my inexperience of normal and not normal I interpreted this as a DANGER and it was a long time before I read in the paddock or let Nugget lay down next to me.

Nugget helping me with the first Pocket Guide

Whether your fear is good or bad will depend upon what it causes you to do.

The consequences of fear on goal achievement

When it comes to having, doing or being whatever it is you are striving to have, do or be, fear is a real bugga-boo. Why? The short and long of the problem rests with the fact that fear stuffs up your ability and/or your willingness to take action.

Fear causes you to replace useful actions that relate to your goal with useless actions that do not make a contribution to learning, change or achievement.

The formula is very simple: If you are unable or unwilling to take useful actions that relate to your goal then there is:

No learning
No change
No achievement
No fun

Full stop.

Fear, therefore, is problematic

There are two distinct ways that fear can, and is, undermining what it is you want to do.

Nugget lying down while I read about what we are supposed to do next. That's not normal!

Problem #1
You cannot find it within yourself to INITIATE actions that count.

For a certainty this is where I was stuck. Fear can utterly and completely block you from being able to take action. For instance, if you have a goal to learn to swim 500m the ONLY way you could utterly fail to succeed is if what you fear causes you to avoid going to the pool.

Fortunately, my first few months were SMOOTH SAILING as a yachty might say. Those few FEAR NOW experiences I did have I was successfully avoiding and not feeling guilty about. There was a lot on my horsemanship plate and I never ran out of things to do. This was also good because I hadn't yet figured out just what bravery was all about. I did not really know what to do with some of the things that were happening to me and if it was not covered in my Level 1 student materials then WHAT WAS I TO DO?

I covered each lesson of Pat's program in turn and my early habit of ANTICIPATING FEAR started to disappear into the back part of my mind. This was good because Helen had bought her own horse, Decker, and Nugget was now MY RESPONSIBILITY.

I did have one problem. I was not gaining much confidence as a rider and this was an important experience because it helped me have to CONFRONT Problem #2 which was timely because that is the next thing to write about in this book.

Problem #2
You cannot find it within yourself to SUSTAIN action long enough to matter.

Fear can cause you to prematurely quit an action before any good learning or change can come from it. In other words, you might muster the courage to get out there and start doing something useful but then fear causes you to stop. Let's say, you get yourself to the pool (initiate the action), but the other swimmers in your lane make you nervous. That fear or concern might cause you to abandon your swimming practice before any learning value is gained.

My lack of confidence as a rider stemmed mostly from the fact that I just couldn't seem to do enough of it.

I would get very nervous whenever Nugget did ANYTHING because I didn't know how to interpret what was happening. If Nugget kicked at a fly on his belly, or bent his head down to scratch his leg, it'd be enough to end a session. In those days I didn't know he was kicking at a fly or scratching his leg. My brain just went DANGER, DANGER! Get out fast.

Some days I would be confident when I got on Nugget, then something would happen and I would just get off and that was ALL SHE WROTE. Some days NEWLY EMERGING ANTICIPATED FEARS limited me to simply getting on and sitting there for an amount of time while Nugget grazed. Then I would get off, take off the saddle and call it a day. On days I was feeling more confident I would ask him to walk a few steps, then stop. Then walk. Then stop. I was very nervous about what might happen if I asked him to turn so I would get off, turn him, then get back on and go back the other way. Trotting was a major event and was limited to only a few rare sessions and only when Helen was there to watch. I was making progress but it was slow and disjointed.

In the end I found myself having the intention of riding for say 30 minutes but I would abandon the session after whatever few minutes it took for me to find a good enough excuse. I was directly and personally experiencing Problem #2. Not sustaining action long enough to make a difference as a rider.

Eventually, these experiences stacked up and I was right back at Problem #1. Not taking any action at all.

So now you know there are the two ways that fear becomes a barrier to doing some of the things you think you want to do. I WANTED to feel what it would feel like to ride Nugget in a canter along a long country road. I WANTED to feel a connection with him while he WORKED A COW (not that I have any idea why I'd wanted to do this, but it looked like people had fun doing it). To do any of this I was going to need:

1. An understanding of the nature of fear so I could make better sense of my experience;
2. Strategies to take action for the sake of learning; and,
3. Strategies to sustain those actions long enough to make a difference.

Fear interferes with useful, positive action replacing it with useless, counterproductive action or no action at all.

Most things we want to accomplish have elements that can stimulate a fear response. When you reach the point that I found myself at there is very little that you can do to change this by simply "thinking about it while sitting on the couch". You will need to take action and therefore you will need strategies to override the natural and normal effects of fear.

I went straight back to the drawing board to sort out what I could do to get myself back out there.

CHAPTER 3

The Transformations of Fear

Clearly fear is problematic. As I previously mentioned fear is a response that is designed to protect you but which can also be counterproductive. Whatever it is that triggers the fear response may not be harmful, or harmful enough to warrant causing us to avoid it. The fear might be irrational or based on faulty information. Of course, there will be times when there is a genuine risk of harm. Often this is caused by our own inexperience. Those fears would change if we could just get passed the avoidance to take action caused by the fear. This is called THE VICIOUS CYCLE OF FEAR.

I kept a journal of my experiences from the time I began

studying Pat's program and playing with Nugget. Three themes emerged in my notes. The first was my ever-present desire that the fear I was feeling about 101 different things would just GO AWAY. There is nothing illogical about hoping that we can eliminate fears that are plaguing our efforts to get where it is we want to go. I knew that for all the riding and playing with horses that people do there just has to be times when they feel nothing. I just cannot imagine Pat feels anything when he picks up his horse's feet. It's a job. He's not saying, "I'm so excited and happy picking up my horse's feet!" GIVE ME A BREAK. Yet I was feeling A LOT of the body of symptoms of fear when I picked up Nugget's feet.

Just as often I wrote about my fascination with people who seemed to genuinely be HAVING FUN. A lot of people were having fun. But clearly they weren't always having fun. I was sure they had had many fears to overcome along the way. I pondered about what in the world I would have to do that could cause me to experience horses and riding as FUN! When you are struggling with fear fun lives on another planet.

I also found a lot of entries in which I wrote about being confused by the people I met who had just as much, and in cases more, fear than I did when they were with their horses but who were out riding their horses on trail rides, cantering around trees and working cows. Things I only dreamed of doing on the days when those dreams didn't cause really BIG ANTICIPATED FEAR responses.

It seemed to me I had three choices. Feel nothing, feel something good, or be afraid and doing it anyway. Observing this I decided that I needed to GET A DOSE OF REALITY about exactly what it was I was trying to do.

I spent a good couple of days thinking about my life experiences where fear had been a factor. Being a nervous sort I had many experiences to choose from. I analysed what happened to those fears as I gained experiences and those previously feared activities came to be a part of my work and personal life. My investigations matched my observations. Sometimes a past fear just went away. Sometimes I somehow learned to enjoy and be excited by something that had previously frightened me. And sometimes the fear just stayed.

The three possible and consistent outcomes

The question is: What can you realistically expect to do with the fear response you have to the many objects, activities, people, places and situations that surround your goals?

Possibility #1
The fear response might neutralise and you will then feel nothing at all

There were many frightening things to do with horses that I had to do as a natural part of being a horse owner. Picking up feet to pick out the hooves, reaching underneath to get hold of the cinch, bandaging an injured leg, worming with a syringe full of paste taken orally, taking his temperature with a thermometer up the hind end. None of these things did I imagine I would want to feel excited about. What I wanted to feel was nothing. They were jobs that would have to be done at times.

When I first started getting on Nugget my biggest FEAR NOW responses came when HE would get a fright. A horse feels like one big contracting muscle when something out of the blue scares them. The entirety of the horse moves at once. First you are here, and then you are two metres over there. Nugget's reactions were mild as horses go in this regard but I just had a lot of trouble dealing with the fear response that this caused in me. The tingles in my skin would take minutes to go away and I wanted to get off. In that way, this was affecting my willingness to sustain the useful action of riding. Eventually, I started anticipating this event before riding and it would affect my willingness to initiate the action of riding in the days to come.

This was a common enough experience that I wanted my fear response to this to neutralise so I felt nothing. I started to play a game called HOW MANY FRIGHTS CAN WE HAVE TODAY. I convinced myself that if I experienced a hundred frights I would eventually get bored with counting them and they would stop causing me to have such a big fear response. Every time he jumped I just counted. That's another one.

I would write in my journal, "We had 3 frights today. 87 to go." Interestingly, I lost count somewhere around 68 because I just stop noticing them as important. When Nugget jumps I feel something but it isn't processed as fear. Instead I feel an "Oh Nugget, you're alright" response.

Having fun or being excited is not always the outcome you will want for the stuff that frightens you. Sometimes the best outcome will be to feel nothing at all.

Possibility #2
The fear response might change to something else.
Such as curiosity, confidence, excitement or fun.

Experiences can most definitely transform a fear response into another emotion. I had had Nugget at home for 8 months and had passed all of my Level 1 tasks when Pat and Linda came to Australia for a visit. I had the good fortune that they chose to stay with me for a couple of days. Pat offered to give Helen and I a lesson and asked us to think about anything that we felt we wanted help with. Oh, the choices! I was riding Nugget but was still very shaky. I was doing as much of what I could do as possible, going a little ways at a trot, stopping, going again, stopping. I never travelled outside of the arena except when Helen offered to give me pony rides by walking in front of Nugget holding the lead rope. Helen in the mean time was already cantering. Clearly, I needed help riding in general.

Helen and I had an early breakfast together and talked about the impending lesson with Pat. I had made myself very nervous by the time Pat and Linda got up. Not so nervous that I was going to finagle my way out of this opportunity. We went through a nerve-wracking first half hour saddling our horses and playing with them on the ground. We learned first hand about what is called THE PAT FACTOR. That is the rapid deterioration of any semblance of SAVVY when Pat is present. Being a VERY GOOD teacher he chatted and spent time looking here and there and that helped TAKE PRESSURE OFF. I felt like a horse in Pat's master horseman's hands.

We walked our horses to the arena and mounted. Pat asked us to do whatever we wanted to do to warm up. He watched us with his energy sucked in so we did not feel the effect of his presence too strongly too soon. We walked, trotted and stopped hither and thither. We backed up and yielded hindquarters and forequarters. I had trouble thinking of things I could do. Our horses kept bumping into each other and I was getting really pissed off at Decker who was ruining my rhythm. It was unusual for Helen and Decker to be in the arena when I rode. It was just TOO MUCH information. I reconciled that I was just going to have to cope with it today. This was not a good time to have a "CONVERSATION" about it with Helen.

Pat watched for quite a time not saying anything. There was the occasional positive nod and smile. Every now and again he turned away from us and talked to Linda for a time and I relaxed a bit when he did that and I think that is why he did that. He then asked us to stop in the middle of the arena side by side.

He got up and started walking toward one of the arena gates while Linda headed for the other. He said he was going to have us do a task. He said, "I am going to open the gates to the arena. I want you to trot for 7 minutes without stopping. You can stay on the arena or go outside. Whatever you feel you want to do. At the end of 7 minutes I want you to finish back in the centre of the arena where you are now." He said this with authority so we understood he really meant it. He was so deadpan I didn't even try to make a joke or explain why that was not really going to be a good idea. I remember chuckling but it was not a YIP-PEE THIS WILL BE FUN kind of chuckle. It was more of a modulated groan.

I looked at Helen with the I'M GOING TO THROW UP look and she gave me the I'M GOING TO STRANGLE YOU AFTER THIS look.

Pat lifted his wrist to look at his watch and he said, "Go." There was nothing we could do but start so off we went. Nugget immediately wanted to tuck in behind Decker. I knew from past experiences that following Decker could be trouble because she goes places she wants to go at a gait faster than I want to ride Nugget. So I rudely steered him away and apologised under my breath. I did that a few more times when he got too near an open gate.

I had continuously trotted longer than I ever had before when Pat yelled out, "12 seconds".

Helen and I both laughed from some fear and much excitement and I said a prayer and we kept going. I am saying over and over, I'M DOING IT. I'M DOING IT.

It does not take long before I am tired from trying to control Nugget's direction and I do not want to be seen to be pulling on his head so much. So I give up and he immediately goes back to following Decker. Decker has by now figured out that she is in control and is determined to get off the arena and out into the paddock. I am really wobbly and yelling at Helen to KEEP CONTROL OF DECKER. I am shouting, "Don't let her go too fast, don't go near the trees, please don't let her break into a canter up that hill." I talked and talked which is what I do when I am out of my comfort zone. The only way I could control my horse was if Helen controlled hers.

As Decker and Nugget are trotting down the small hill toward the arena I am thinking surely this is it, Pat yells, "One minute forty-five seconds." We had already been everywhere there is to go on my small property twice. Most of which I had never ridden on before except with my trusty pony-ride operator Helen.

There was nothing to do but to continue following Decker wherever she decided to go because by this time we were way out of Helen's range of experience and she stopped trying to steer and was just hanging on for the ride. I forget about trying to look cool in front of Pat and I keep pulling on Nugget's head because the reins were my way of keeping my balance. This is not my walk, trot, stop routine.

Then, all of a sudden everything in my brain went very quiet. I was not afraid and being off balance did not feel as bad as it had just a minute before. I had gone long enough that my brain had figured some things out, GOOD LITTLE BRAIN.

It was ugly but for the last couple of minutes I was trotting and thinking about other things at the same time. This was quite an amazing feeling. It was near the end and I had lived and felt quite exhilarated. Finally, Pat announces, "Six minutes, thirty seconds." He instructs us to head back into the arena and to stop in the middle with our horses facing him. This meant we should be facing him too.

We stopped and I am covered in sweat. This was an awesome experience. I had just done something I would not or could not have gotten myself to do in a hundred riding sessions on my own.

What I remember is sitting for a long time in the middle of the arena SOAKING on this experience. I do not know what Pat thought. He seemed happy that we had finished the task. I did not quit and I believe he knew just how hard this was for me to do, for both of us to do. The session ended with Helen and I jabbering nonsense and with a new goal set by Pat that we were to work toward in our future riding sessions. That goal was to trot for 21 minutes without stopping. When we achieved that goal we were to call him to tell him. I was energised but still raw from the 7 minute experience. 21 minutes seemed like a big leap, but possible.

Pat says, "Horses teach riders". I knew this concept but I was having trouble experiencing what it really meant in the saddle. I hoped that the path to achieving the new goal would cause me to finally eradicate the fear I was still feeling as a rider. Already the fears I felt riding, at least on our property, had transformed.

I was ready to take this experience and continue on my own but the next morning Linda woke up full of fire about an idea she'd had. She had been developing a concept called "fluidity" to help riders get in harmony with their horses. It was still a new concept and the process of developing fluidity hadn't been tried on many people. The idea was to try to teach this to us in the time we had left together, about an hour. I learned many months later that what Linda saw in my riding scared her and provided the motivation for this experience.

In the hour before I had to take Pat and Linda to the airport to fly back to America, I went and got Nugget ready while Pat and Helen made spareribs to eat on the trip. We all started in the gym with a quick session using the Swiss exercise ball and sitting on each other's backs where I learned what a horse feels when I do what I do while riding. POOR NUGGET.

We then headed to the arena where I got on Nugget. I was given instructions to put my reins on Nugget's withers and my hands over the reins PUSHING my weight down into my hands. Linda then asked me to do a PASSENGER LESSON. This is where Nugget's responsibility is to maintain whatever gait I ask for but he can go wherever he wants to go. If he changes gait I let him and then lift the rein on one side asking him politely to GET BACK WITH THE PROGRAM. I am not allowed to change his direction unless he is taking me into a tree. I asked for a trot and off we went. I immediately, and I mean instantly, felt balanced and for the first time. I wasn't going anywhere. This was MAGICAL. I needed no reins for balance and I could FEEL Nugget's movement. I felt SAFE! I just went where he went however he got there. If he jigged I jigged. If he stopped quickly so did I. It was just NO BIG DEAL. Literally harmony. I was chuckling for what chuckling is for, to express joy. I felt safe.

Linda said I could go as long as I wanted. When I looked at my watch I had already been trotting for nearly 7 minutes. It was easy. I was going everywhere with Nugget. Up hills, on the arena, off the arena and even near the trees. I felt fantastic and I did not want to stop EVER but the spareribs and ride to the airport beckoned. My fear response to riding Nugget in this context had now changed forever.

There will be times when, like my experiences on these two days with Pat and Linda, your experiences will cause a fundamental change in your fear response.

As an aside, you will find when this happens it is near impossible to go backwards and almost instantly you will forget that you were ever afraid of this thing, or person, or place or activity. Amnesia is a part of learning.

The next morning I woke up, got Nugget and headed out for my second pushing passenger lesson at the trot. Four days later I had trotted for 21 minutes and made my call to Pat.

A nice moment with Nugget after the session with Pat and Linda

Possibility #3
The fear response might continue
You will need strategies to feel the fear response
but take action anyway.

Believe it or not, there will be times when having the fear response stay intact is not such a bad idea. As mentioned earlier, fear can lead you to be more vigilant and disciplined. When there is a real risk of injury involved in what you are doing I think keeping the fear response is a good thing.

In some cases, however, even if fear is not really needed or wanted no amount of action will change or neutralise it. The response might lessen in its intensity but it remains.

For instance, I have been lecturing to audiences since very early in my career. The stage fright I get before going on stage is still, after all these years, very strong. I have joked that I'd rather be shot than get on stage. Of course, once I am there I would rather be shot than get off! I have never been able to change or neutralise the emotional response to standing up to present a lecture. I have had to learn coping strategies to enable me to feel those feelings but get up to perform anyway.

In this case, this fear while uncomfortable is a good one to keep. What is good about this fear continuing is that is causes my brain and body to get in the heightened state needed to perform. It also causes me to be very disciplined in my preparations.

Fortunately, at the level of horsemanship I was working on I didn't have any fear response that didn't change or neutralise with experience. By the time I did I had found the BRAVERY STRATEGY I talk about in the second part of this book. As you will discover I needed it.

If you reflect on your own life experiences you will no doubt find that you have had each of these changes to fear responses many times. Some fears changed, some stopped and some continue no matter what you have tried. Each in its own way is a good outcome.

Do not expect to have control over the outcome you get

It is important to know now that you might not have control over the kind of change that occurs to your fear responses. Some things, like my response to Nugget's frights, might never neutralise no matter how much I might wish for it or work on it. If that turns out to be the case, I need to reconcile that this is just what it is and ensure I have a BRAVERY STRATEGY to see that it does not get in the way of the progress in my studies or pursuit of riding for pleasure.

My one conclusion

I wrote at the start of this chapter that I had found three possible outcomes (the fear can transform, neutralise or remain) and one conclusion.

The one CONCLUSION I came to was this: My current fear responses would never neutralise or change if I did not have strategies to take action while I am still feeling the fear. Fear was not just going to GO AWAY by itself. Why would it? Your brain believes it's doing the RIGHT THING.

What you want to control is not what the fear will change to, but your ability to motivate yourself to take action no matter what the outcome turns out to be. Nothing changes without action so the control you want is over the actions you take. Doing this allows you to continue on the path to achieving your goal.

That same action is what is necessary for the fear to transform or for you to learn to cope with it if it persists.

It is time to take a look at what is meant by the term BRAVERY.

CHAPTER 4

Just What is Bravery?

Imagine the consequence if your brain used only the emotion of fear to support its decisions about what you would or would not do. You would be stifled at nearly every turn. If fear were the dominant emotion driving what humans did and did not do there would be no exploration, experimentation, adaptation or improvement. No climbing mountains, no exploring the seas. There would be no new medicines and no new procedures. Put simply, there would be no forward movement or progress.

How many things in your own life have you accomplished because you somehow figured out a way to take action even when you knew in advance you would experience fear? How many times have you advanced on some goal because you did not quit when you started to be afraid? I know in my own life I would not have written a book, ridden a motorcycle, completed my PhD, had pets, taught teenagers and prisoners, started my own business, moved to Australia, defended myself against detractors, or met some of my current friends. I most certainly would not have had the experiences with horses I needed to have to work with Pat and Linda. What a loss to my life that would have been.

We have all accomplished goals, some big, some small that required us to overcome some element of fear or concern. Sometimes the circumstances are just right and we make it. Other times they do not and we fail. Few of us have control over this aspect of achievement unless we have learned strategies to control our own behaviour.

If we want to increase our odds for success we need to learn strategies that allow us to be in conscious control of our behaviour because the HEART of this issue is this: To wilfully engage in an activity that is frightening is NOT normal human behaviour. It is exceptional.

>*Bravery is the KEY factor*
>*in this exceptional behaviour.*

I was going to need this exceptional behaviour for my next step on my horsemanship path.

What exactly is bravery?

By now you understand that avoiding actions that will lead to a fear response is NORMAL. It would be normal to avoid travelling if you have a fear of flying. In the same way it would be normal to avoid friends who might ask you to travel if you have a fear of flying.

The World Veteran's Track and Field Championships were held in Puerto Rico in July 2003. I have been sprinting for many years and felt I was up for the challenge. I made a commitment to go to the Championships. This commitment was actually a good PSYCHOLOGICAL TRICK I was playing on myself to get back to the US. I had been procrastinating over a trip home for 10 years.

Given that Colorado can be seen as ON THE WAY HOME to Australia from Puerto Rico the door was open to accepting the invitation extended by Pat and Linda to visit them at the *Pat Parelli Center* in Pagosa Springs, Colorado. Making a trip solely for the purpose of playing with horses would have been hard to justify especially as I was still searching for the meaning of horses in my life.

I planned for a 5 week visit knowing that horses and horsemanship challenges would be IN THE CARDS. Helen, my security blanket, was coming along too. From the comfort zone of MY little property in MY now well-honed routine on MY familiar horse I really knew that I JUST WAS NOT READY. There were so many things that caused an ANTICIPATED FEAR RESPONSE I had no real minutes to find anything to feel excited about.

After my lessons the previous year with Pat and Linda I progressed well with Nugget. Pushing passenger lessons came easier and went for longer. Being a new rider, I spent a lot of time using the pushing passenger lessons because they were what I could now do confidently. But there is one thing about experiences like the ones I had with Pat and Linda that day back in November. They do cause a fear response to change in a positive direction but the consequence of that is that you ADVANCE and then you find a whole new set of things to be afraid of!

At the *Pat Parelli Center* I would to have to meet, play with and ride a strange horse. I would have to ride in a different saddle. I would be attending classes with other people who all sat on horses near one another. This is something I had avoided AT ALL COSTS from the time I sent Helen off to that first clinic with Nugget. I knew there would be a lot of attention on me and I was afraid I was going to look like an idiot. THEN there was the knowledge that Pat and Linda had PLANS FOR US. I kept flashing on the experience of sitting in our arena being tasked to trot for 7 minutes. This was going to be WAY OVER THE TOP. I was not feeling anything that resembled brave.

Bravery is often perceived as something you are either born with or not. Like an attribute you should JUST HAVE IN YOUR KIT, and people who have it do not understand people who don't. If you don't, you're just stuck.

Willpower is closely associated with bravery and is perceived in this same way too. Many people have been taught and believe that a person who procrastinates or who doesn't do what they said they would is lazy, slack or undisciplined. They think, "If only YOU had willpower!" or "If only I had willpower!" But what is willpower? Is it some innate ability given to some and not to others?

No, it isn't.

Willpower, like bravery, is a set of strategies that enables a person to take action. Where willpower strategies enable you to take actions that are boring, frustrating or are otherwise unpleasant, bravery enables you to take actions that are frightening. Someone called a PROCRASTINATOR is someone who has never been taught willpower strategies. Someone called a

WIMP is someone who has never been taught a strategy to be BRAVE.

Bravery is a strategy you can learn to use to override your protective brain when it is overreacting or is otherwise in the way of getting where you want to go.

A bravery strategy enables you to STAY IN THE GAME. It enables you to take another step toward something in which fear is interfering.

If fear is blocking your motivation or ability to take action in order to achieve a goal, then it is a bravery strategy that will get you out there.

After 15 months on this horsemanship adventure I had encountered more than a few things that required a bravery strategy to stay in the game. But studying in the privacy of my own little world meant I could avoid those activities! Fortunately, horsemanship has many facets and I was never terminally stuck. I always had something I could do to STAY IN THE HORSE GAME.

But the trip to the U.S. changed all that. In the days leading up to the planned trip my brain was working overtime trying to come up with a good enough excuse to skip over Colorado without feeling guilty and not looking like a WIMP. I needed an excuse that if I told others and myself would allow me to feel okay about myself. I did not have any luck. No matter what I came up with I still felt guilty and wimpy.

I needed a bravery strategy to get on the plane to America.

CHAPTER 5

Reality Test

Changing a fear response or learning to cope with it is always a challenge. But far less a challenge if you can get clear about what it is that is truly triggering the fear response and an honest sense of JUST HOW BAD it really is or isn't.

MOVE CLOSER
STAY LONGER

Step 1

The first step I took was to think about the triggers for my fears IN CONTEXT. This means not only identifying WHAT I am afraid of, but as importantly in what SITUATIONS SPECIFICALLY I am afraid. Saying, "I am afraid to ride" was not useful. It is too general and also was not true! In some situations

I felt quite confident to ride. Saying instead, "I am afraid to ride alone" was far more useful and it was true. I could work with that!

You probably already know the people, places, objects, situations and tasks that you find frightening. For you it might be "your boss", "dogs", "giving a speech", "picking up your horse's feet" or "driving on the highway". But simply identifying the fear is not necessarily useful. What makes the information about your fears useful is when you identify the situation in which the fear is triggered and situations in which it isn't or is but less intensely. You might say, "it's my boss in the Friday review meeting", or "dogs running loose in the neighbourhood when I am riding my motorcycle", or "John Smith's dog."

I recorded my fears surrounding the trip to Pagosa Springs and I paid attention to details of context. I wrote that I was afraid of being "on a horse near other people on horses in a SMALL space", "given a NERVOUS horse to ride", "given a BIG horse to ride", "given an English saddle to use", "asked to do something I was afraid to do or did not know how to do in front of other people."

This caused me to feel VERY DIFFERENTLY than when my thoughts were turning on generalities. IT GAVE ME SOMETHING TO WORK ON!

This is CRITICAL INFORMATION because it does three very important things.

Important thing #1
My fears were related to specific situations

It helped me see I was not afraid in general, I was afraid of specific situations. It helped me KNOW EXACTLY what was what with my fears. This specificity helps my brain to help me focus on solving the actual problems. And, importantly, I found the list to be quite short and manageable when compared to the whole list of other things I would be doing with Pat and Linda.

Important thing #2
I couldn't know exactly what I might confront

Only if I found myself in the situation of having a nervous horse would I THEN need to do something to help me take useful actions. I did not need to be afraid YET of what I could not know.

Important thing #3
I was making up a LOT of stuff in my head

Why would I be thinking that Pat or Linda would give me a nervous horse to ride? This is called a MIND BOGGLER or more simply DUMB.

Take the time to find out more about your fears. If you have a fear of speaking in front of others then discover whether that fear is more or less dependent upon specific things, such as: the size of the audience; who's in the audience; the topic; the location; having to wear a microphone; and so on.

If you have a fear of skiing discover if the fear is present in all or only some specific conditions like when you can't see due to falling snow, or when the snow is hard packed. Is there a specific time of day, or group of people that cause skiing to be more, or less frightening.

If you are afraid of a particular person is the fear intensity the same if you visit that individual in person or talk to them on the phone.

Your first step is to gather as much information about your fears in context as you can.

Step 2

By having identified what people, places, objects, situations and tasks trigger a fear response, and importantly, in what specific situations, you have made important and useful distinctions. You now need to know what specifically you can do without help and what you will need a bravery strategy to do. The second step is to CATEGORISE your fears by making three lists.

List #1	**List #2**	**List #3**
What CAN YOU DO, and in what situation, and feel no negative emotion	What CAN YOU DO, and in what situation, even though you feel a little fearful	What CAN'T YOU DO, and in what situation because the feeling of fear is too intense.

My list looked something like:

List #1 What CAN I DO and in what situation and feel no fear	**List #2** What CAN I DO and in what situation even though I feel a little fearful	**List #3** What CAN'T I DO and in what situation because the feeling of fear is too intense.
• I can ride Nugget when Helen is riding Decker. • I can brush and groom Nugget. • Nugget and I can do all of the tasks in Level 1 and 2 on the ground and at liberty, and all of the riding tasks in Level 1 and everything in Level 2 up to stage 4.	• I can ride Nugget anywhere on my property. • I can stand up in the stirrups at the walk. • I can follow the rail at a walk and trot. • I can do an emergency dismount. • I can ride with 1 rein in my small arena.	• I cannot pick up Nugget's hind feet. • I cannot brush Nugget's tail. • I cannot stand directly behind Nugget. • I cannot canter. • I cannot allow Nugget to walk over even a small log. • I cannot blanket Nugget since his big fright. • I cannot think about riding another horse. • I cannot stand up in the stirrups at the trot. • I cannot think about being on a horse surrounded by other people on horses. • I cannot ride with 1 rein outside the arena.

Keep your lists handy. Add to them as new information comes to light. The GAME you will play with the bravery strategy is move the people, places, objects, situations and tasks on your third list in to your second list.

Step 3

This step is easy. Take the actions you can take. Repetition and experience is the key to the items on List #2. These items are just crying out for more action. This is the path of moving the items on this list to List #1. The items on your first list are where your confidence resides. Doing those items frequently ensures you spend time being conscious of the things you can do. There is no doubt some of those items were at one time on List #2 or List #3. They should remind you that you HAVE MADE changes. Everything on my List #1 was at one time on the third list. This is very motivating and that in goal achievement IS the reward.

Make plans to do as many repetitions of the activities on List #1 and 2.

Step 4

It is the items you have identified and placed on List #3 which disclose what is currently standing between you and reaching the next stage of your goal!

Perhaps one or more of these items are even standing in the way of achieving the goal altogether!

The bravery strategy is about enabling you to INITIATE actions that you cannot or will not do because of the intensity of your ANTICIPATED FEAR RESPONSE. It is also about enabling you to SUSTAIN these actions long enough to have a positive impact on the intensity of the fear response.

There are two edges related to the fears on List #3. One edge of the fear response is defined by how CLOSE YOU CAN GET to the thing that triggers the fear BEFORE the fear response starts. Close is defined by time or distance. The other edge is defined by how close you can get in time or distance before the feeling is so strong that you HAVE to retreat.

As noted above, CLOSE can relate to time and distance (space). For example, I have no fear about attending a horsemanship clinic two months before it is scheduled but a week before it starts the sensations begin. And I do not feel a fear sensation with a dog when it is across the street. But I cannot make myself walk on the same side of the street without a strong reaction.

Step 4 is not a difficult process and it is a crucial one. Once you clearly identify the two edges of your fear response you will be ready to get on with the process of transforming these fears.

Edge #1
How close is close enough

One edge of the fear response is defined by how CLOSE YOU CAN GET to the thing that triggers the fear BEFORE THE FEAR RESPONSE STARTS.

Edge #2
How close is too close

The second edge is defined by how close you can get before the feeling is so strong that you JUST HAVE to move away.

We arrived in Pagosa Springs in the middle of July. We were taken on a tour of the ranch spanning 700 acres that contained everything a student horseman might wish for. Covered arenas, immaculate grounds, big open arenas, tack rooms convenient to the horse yards, mountains for trail riding, open meadows and people doing interesting things with horses. Everything about it was beautiful and everywhere we went I met someone I had met before on my *Parelli* adventure in Australia. I felt as if I were coming home.

Two horses had been selected for us and our tack was already in the tack room. We were anxious to get to know our equine partners for this part of our adventure. I went to the yards and met a large brown quarter horse named Buddy who looked like a large version of Nugget, while Helen introduced herself to PacMan.

The first invitation we received to be tasked was from Linda. She suggested we might like to participate on the ground in her new Level 3 class. This was fun and I felt very successful and confident with Buddy.

A few days later it was time for the class to meet with horses saddled over at one of the two large playgrounds. With Linda's permission and under her watchful eye we were allowed to saddle up and participate where we could on the fringe of the class.

THIS WAS IT!

The playground incorporated a very large round yard in which four smaller round yards were contained. This is called a CLOVERLEAF and it is good for many horsemanship tasks and accommodates teaching groups. I had already played with Buddy on the ground and found him to be calm and responsive. I, however, had not yet ridden Buddy and two of my worst ANTICIPATED FEARS were about to become a FEAR NOW experience. I would be riding Buddy, an unfamiliar horse, for the first time AND with other people on horses around me.

Standing outside the cloverleaf at the start of class with Linda

When we arrived Linda briefed us. She suggested to anyone who was nervous or unconfident that they go inside one of the small round yards inside the cloverleaf. I weighed up my fears and found I had less fear of looking like an idiot than of the other people on horses so I made a beeline for the small yard nearest me while waving my hand at Linda saying, "Me, me, me". I was comforted to find the other three small round yards occupied by other riders. It meant I might not be the only unconfident rider in the class.

Being inside the small, enclosed round yard where other horses couldn't come near left me with no real fear except the one I had about riding an unfamiliar horse. Linda set the class a riding task that I didn't really hear for the noise in my head. I decided to get to know Buddy and started on my own task again with disregard for what anyone thought, a Pushing Passenger

Lesson. He was very easy to ride and more comfortable to ride than Nugget. Within a few minutes I was caught up to the class doing the assigned task in my protected space. Already one of my fears on my third list was on the move to List #2.

I was nervous whenever I looked out at the gaggle of other riders even though I wasn't out there with them. The other students were all laughing and joking around without a care. To me it looked like an accident just about to happen. It made my stomach do flip-flops. How did they do it?

After a while Linda offered students who felt confident to leave the cloverleaf enclosure to continue the task outside in the playground. Some people took her up on this while others did not. This thinned out the crowd. The outer area within the cloverleaf looked less fearful to me with what seemed enough room to avoid others so I ventured out of my little round enclosure. This was a big step and I was proud of myself. It reminded me of graduating to BIG SCHOOL.

It took only a minute or two to get used to the new environment. Not much time passed before I was kind of confidently riding with a few other riders around the big round yard.

Then Linda called all the students back inside the cloverleaf. I thought I could stay out there and I tried to for as long as I could stand it. It was not long before I was totally overwhelmed and overloaded. It was either a case of get off and quit or move further away by going back to the comfort of one of the small round yards. I quickly BEAT A PATH to the security of my small and EMPTY space.

This was a very big success. First, I could go back to the place I was staying and update my lists. I CAN ride another horse and FEEL ONLY A LITTLE FEAR. I CAN ride with other people around me if there are only a few of them. I was also able to add to List #3. I CANNOT ride a new horse out in the big open playground. I CANNOT ride a horse when there are more riders than there is room for me to move far enough away. And so on.

I had found the edges of the RIDING WITH OTHERS item on List #3. I knew more about this fear. I knew how close I could get before the FEAR NOW response started, Edge #1. And I knew how close was too close causing me to not be able to go further because of the intensity of the FEAR NOW response, Edge #2. Armed with this I could begin to make plans to work on this.

There will be times when the edge of your fear relates not to space, how physically close, but instead to time.

I can be a nervous passenger on a plane but interestingly I do not have any fear response whatsoever when booking trips to other cities for work or pleasure. I usually do this many months in advance of the trip. However, I am notorious for cancelling plans especially if they are for pleasure. As it gets closer to the TIME to make the trip I start having an ANTICIPATED FEAR RESPONSE. It's small at first and gets worse as the time draws near. I can shrug off the early concerns but it gets harder when I start waking in the night with worry and I have unbidden images of planes in distress popping into my mind. This is when, if I can cancel, I do.

The same is true with lecturing. I happily book to do lectures each year for organisations but as the time gets closer to delivering the lecture the intensity of the ANTICIPATED FEAR RESPONSE escalates. I can be a total wreck just before going on.

The closer it gets the more intense it is. You might notice that you make plans to do things easily but then as it gets closer to the time to take action you begin looking for good enough

[Handwritten at top: Trust issue first not really fear]

reasons to put it off.

Now you know a little about the effect of spatial or time proximity on your emotions in general and of fear specifically. You want to know where the first and second edges are for all those people, places, objects, situations and tasks that right now interfere with whatever it is you are trying to accomplish.

Understanding your lists in relation to the edges

Some very important lessons can now be brought into focus about the people, places, objects, situations and tasks that you identified and put on your 3 lists.

The items on your first list that include things you can do and feel no fear. They have NEITHER Edge #1 or #2. You can get as close as you like and stay as long as you like with no fear response.

The items on your second list that include things you can do even though you feel fear have an Edge #1 but DO NOT have an Edge #2. There is a closeness in either time or in space at which you feel the FEAR NOW response start, and that feeling gets more intense as you get closer. But it never gets so strong that you have to abandon the action.

Then, there are the items on your third list that include things you can't do because the feelings are just too intense. These fears have BOTH edges. There is a definite place in time or space when the fear response starts and there is a definite place in space and time where you cannot go further forward because the feeling is too intense.

This is what makes the items on List #3 so important to identify. It is these that interfere most with your achievements. They are certainly the most difficult to deal with.

It is probably a good time to now define the edges of the fears you identified and wrote on your third list. Remember you have 2 things to discover.

> *How close are you, in time or space, when the fear response starts?*

> *How close can you get before the feeling is too strong to stay?*

What you are aiming to do?

The work you do as a result of this chapter will be very illuminating. You will learn important things about fear and may be surprised by the things you learn about yourself.

When I am striving for an important goal I look at this often as old fears are transformed and new ones emerge in relation to my next set of challenges. Before I did this exercise my ANTICIPATED FEARS related to going to be with Pat and Linda in Colorado felt all encompassing.

What was I afraid of for real? There was no way I could know without doing some discovery. Then, armed with the awareness I gained I was quickly able to use the bravery strategy to get past most everything that was standing in the way of my progress at that time.

Everything that was scary then is not scary now, and the bits that still have niggles I can cope with while taking more action. They have moved to List #2. In time they will diminish too and shift to List #1. Then, I'll be ready for the next challenges. I don't want to predict what I will find next on my third list. Why worry now about something I'll surely worry about later.

Do this well and you will truly open up the opportunity to get past your fears and get where it is you want to go.

It's your turn now. When you have your lists and have defined the edges for what you write on List #3 you'll be ready to learn the bravery strategy to tackle the items.

The Bravery Strategy

CHAPTER 6

Move Closer Stay Longer

Your ability and willingness to take action is THE essential requirement for you to get where it is you want to go in relation to your goal. The actions that matter in transforming fear are those that cause fear to occur.

I really began to understand that this was how Helen had gained so much confidence when Nugget first came home. I would ask her how in the world could she be out there brushing his tail. She told me that in the beginning she could not do it at all as going anywhere past his withers caused her to feel way too nervous. Her strategy was to go comfortably where she could go and then go a step further until she could feel the discomfort rise up. She said that she then just stayed there in that one spot until the feeling went away. The next day she could quickly go to her new confidence spot and would move further. She was desensitising herself to this task with the goal of brushing Nugget's tail in her mind. Of course, spending this time helped her learn about Nugget and his reactions. He too was being desensitised to her moving along his body with the brush. This solution that Helen adopted is called MOVING CLOSER and STAYING LONGER.

To cause a fundamental change in your emotional response means taking yourself to the place where the fear can be felt, and then staying there long enough for a change to start taking place. This is the outcome for using the *MOVE CLOSER, STAY LONGER* strategy. You have to give your brain and body time to sort things out IN THE SITUATION that is causing a fear response.

By the time I arrived at the *Center* after all the nonsense I put myself through to get there I had made a commitment that I was going to take this unique opportunity to make progress. I was never going to feel less fear if I didn't allow myself to feel something.

By this time I had Nugget for nearly 15 months. In that time I had made what seemed to me to be very little change. I say that because I still could only do very little because I was too afraid to do many things. I had passed Level 1 in the *Parelli* program that focused on safety and communication with your horse. I was a good example of a Level 1 graduate but I was still limited to riding at a walk and trot in a relatively small area. I was not comfortable being around other riders.

To my advantage I did have A LOT ON MY PLATE. Just having a horse to care for was a big deal and there were just things I had no choice but to do. I did slowly gain confidence and there were some big FEAR NOW events to overcome. Like the time Nugget kicked out when I held his back foot for the farrier. Being a new rider meant that just getting on and moving took all my fortitude. But to say I was using what I know about learning and achievement just would not be true.

The first real and perhaps only time I moved close enough to feel the fear and stay long enough for it to change was the day Pat tasked us to trot for 7 minutes. This woke me up and I did continue moving closer and staying longer. All the way to 21 minutes and doing pushing passenger lessons all around the property. But after that, lack of opportunity and imagination caused me to simply repeat over and over again what I was already comfortable doing.

Now, back at the *Pat Parelli Center*, ever so slowly over the next few days I took myself out of the small round yard in the centre of the cloverleaf to participate. Each day I CONSCIOUSLY moved Buddy and myself closer to the other students while they sat on and rode their horses. Each day I moved close enough to feel that sweaty, tight feeling of fear rising. Not so close that it made me want to throw up, just close enough to feel SOMETHING.

Sometimes it was a task given to the class by Linda that expanded my bubble about being near other people on horses. In one session we were asked to face another rider and trot forward passing close enough to give a HIGH 5. We then backed our horses up until they were side by side. We then side passed toward each other until our stirrups touched. This brought fear to life fully in my body. It should. I was on the inside of that first edge. But I wasn't so close that I felt a need to quit.

In less than ONE week I was as comfortable as anyone else

in my class being surrounded by and doing things with other riders. I even did my first trail ride firmly squeezed in between two other horses. I chose to be squeezed between two instructors who were travelling at the end of the pack. That was close enough to feel nervous, but I stayed and by the end of the ride the fear response was negligible.

There were situations like squeezing through a tight space next to someone and some riders, or being near the woman with the horse that kept pinning its ears and reaching out for a bite that caused the intensity of the fear to rise too high for me causing me to want to CALL IT A DAY. But when that happened I took one step back, and then another until I could still feel the fear response but not to the degree where I felt a need to quit. Some situations with horses are a real danger and different situations required different degrees of closeness. To stand next to some riders and their horses always caused a strong fear response in me. IT SHOULD HAVE. Fear is not bad.

Some horses felt a fear response rise in our tasks too and when this happened I watched them take a step back, then back another in search of comfort or the place they could get to where the feeling was just a little less intense. This was just what I was doing.

What is SO important to understand is that what I did not do was stay on the outside of the edge where fear begins to build. And I did not retreat at the first inkling of a sensation. I felt it and I stayed long enough to feel a change even if that change was only that I stayed a little longer this time or it felt just a little less worse than it did at the start.

If I had stayed inside my little round yard away from others, sure I would have felt confident, but that was not ever going to make me more confident or FEEL NOTHING in the presence of other riders. If I could not ride comfortably with other riders I would be forever limited in what fun and excitement having and riding a horse is all about. There would be no clinics, no trail rides and no friends.

Stephanie Burns

CHAPTER 7

Common Mistakes

Move closer, stay longer is a strategic approach to transforming fear responses. Curiosity is nature's support for humans and animals alike to grow increasingly comfortable in new situations and unfamiliar territory. It takes a degree of interest and necessity to drive curiosity. Most of our chosen goals come about because of an interest or necessity. What undermines achievement is a lack of knowing how to ensure you progress. Your actions can just as soon lead you to no progress as good progress. You can even go backwards. Zero progress is a dead end for achievement. Eventually you get bored or too scared and quit. Action for action sake may not lead to change. And experiences do not lead to learning unless they are the right kinds of experiences.

There are three fast paths to failure with the *MOVE CLOSER, STAY LONGER* strategy. These mistakes are made so often it is a wonder we do not learn faster how to avoid them. When I reflect on my past goal pursuits it is clear the many times I made these mistakes and quit. Of course, being a clever human I was able to convince myself I never really wanted the goal in the first place. So, I never learned.

Get to know these pitfalls carefully. They're scattered everywhere on the path to achievement where fear is involved.

Mistake #1
Not getting close enough

In order for you to grow, learn or change you need to get close enough to stimulate the fear response. If you do not get close enough to feel it, there is no opportunity for your brain to learn.

In the end nothing about riding in the confines of an arena could prepare me for riding out in an open space. Arenas can only get SO BIG before they stop being arenas.

After 3 weeks I still had not ventured outside of the enclosed round yards and arenas. I was also getting bored with the repetition of things I could do there, not that there are not a million other things to do there. And I was getting annoyed seeing other people coming and going comfortably on their horses all around the ranch. I got off to walk to the house, while Pat (and Helen) rode. Helen in the meantime is riding comfortably out in the big play yards and around the main buildings at the *Center* and around the pond. But she too had not yet ventured outside the gates into the big open paddocks.

Any THOUGHT of taking Buddy outside the arena and into the open was past my second edge of fear so I felt stuck. I was not getting close enough to cause a change because I didn't know what the first *MOVE CLOSER, STAY LONGER* action might be.

We talked about this over dinner with Pat and Linda and I did not get any closer to an answer. Before we left that night Pat suggested that we might like to go on a trail ride with him the next day. This was a very special opportunity that few people would ever have. We said, "Yes, yes, yes". He told us to meet him down at *Pat's World*, his personal place where he goes each day to work with his top students. We said, "Great" and headed back to the apartment.

Now, we'd been to *Pat's World* several times. It was a bit too far to comfortably walk so we always drove the car there. It suddenly dawned on us that in order to meet Pat at *Pat's World* in the morning with our horses meant either walking the horses there, which would be very embarrassing and slow, or figuring out how to put Buddy in the car which was just plain silly.

The next morning we got to the house very early so we could prepare the horses and ourselves for the trip. To watch us you would have thought we had been tasked to ride over the Rocky Mountains.

I got on Buddy and Helen climbed on PacMan and we were off. We took what I called the OVER THE LOGS ROUTE (these were long poles lying on the ground lining the driveway!) and onto the road to the main gate. I was nervous as hell but managed to feel a twinge of excitement when I noticed other people noticing me out there in the open. If they only knew just how big this was.

Our first challenge came quickly, just 20 metres into the trip. How do we open the gate? I waited at a safe distance while Helen rode PacMan up to the gate where she found a button.

That first millisecond of being on the other side of the gate was awesome. I felt like I was really riding a horse. We were just standing still but this was MOVING CLOSE ENOUGH to feel, and so close that I had to go back. As the main part of the *Center* disappeared behind us I understood for the first time why people ride horses. It was awesome. After having Buddy walk for a few minutes, the fears melted significantly, and my watch told me we were going to be late. We asked our horses to trot. There we were, out in the big world, trotting down a country road with enough fear sensations to let us know we were alive but not enough to entertain a thought about stopping.

My first steps outside of an arena

This experience, coupled with the amazing experiences on the trail ride itself, opened up a whole new world of challenges of riding outside the arena. For the rest of the days we were at the ranch I could go out and find the edge of my fear and stay with it long enough to experience a change. By the end of our stay we rode everywhere there was to ride.

Sometimes you need help from someone else when you cannot tell yourself if you are ready to take the first *MOVE CLOSE ENOUGH* step. Pat had been watching us ride and he knew our horses were confident. Pat has a clever way of making suggestions for one thing that in order to achieve accomplishes something else altogether. Without it at that time I might still be riding in the arena waiting for that outer edge of my fear to ride outside to subside.

You have to get close enough to feel fear rise or there will be no change.

The freedom of the open spaces

Mistake #2
Getting too close

As you have likely gathered, Helen has been the crash test dummy for much of this adventure. Without her on this project it would never have come to anything. She just has an instinct for moving closer and staying long enough. She is also high on the sensation-thrill seeking scale. I took the sensation-thrill seeking test once and when my test was scored and the results graph returned to me, my line was BELOW the bottom edge of the graph.

When I set up hot fence tape in the pasture (this is tape with an electrical current running through it) I asked Helen to test it, which she did by TOUCHING IT. It makes her shake all over and giggle. I, on the other hand, have to move far away from her when she does this and cannot watch. That is how much fear HER doing this causes in ME. Crazy isn't it.

One day I had a new stretch of paddock that needed hot taping. I got everything set up and then sent Helen off to test it. She took a breath in readiness for the jolt, then reached out and grabbed the tape. Her head whip-lashed backwards and she was knocked flat on the ground. She'd had her other hand touching the metal gate.

She misses the sensation of being shocked but has since resorted to using an electronic tester. It will be interesting to see how she is going to *MOVE CLOSER, STAY LONGER* her way over this fear.

The trick is to get close enough to feel the sensation, but not so close that it becomes overwhelming. Do not go too far, too soon, and end up having to quit prematurely or altogether.

Mistake #3
Leaving too soon

Once you are close enough to feel the sensation, you must then be able to stay long enough to give your brain and body a chance to adapt to this stimulus. The third mistake people make is they leave too soon. They do not stay until the sensation changes even a little. By leaving early the fear may even become more intense and they will likely not be able to get as close again the next time. In other words, the first edge will now be further away.

This was the mistake I made with cantering. Cantering was in itself a big deal. There is a moment when you feel ready and you just have to jump at it. This time for me came in Linda's Level 2 class when everyone was given a chance to canter alone in the round corral. I went along with everyone else and finally asked her if it was okay to do this as I had never asked a horse to canter before. It was a huge feeling to manage. I went a short way and as I got wobbly or tight Buddy slowed to a stop. I went again and again. I finally made it one complete lap and rode to the centre of the round corral, stopped and cheered in celebration. I had cantered.

Stopping in the middle of the round yard to celebrate my first canter! I had borrowed Helen's horse PacMan for this experience.

Over the next couple of days I took myself off to the round yard for more practice. Going around in the round corral, even though it was big, was hard work. You are in one big turn and I was not getting more relaxed. I was just doing a bit because I knew this was good but I was stopping while still at the height of discomfort, and usually because the discomfort was getting worse. This is the reverse of what I needed to be doing.

I talked about this with Pat and Linda again over a meal and told them my strategy was to do this everyday I was there knowing that EVENTUALLY the fear response to this would go away. But it was going to take a long time the way I was going. Pat offered to do a cantering lesson the next day and told us to meet him early at *Pat's World*. Fortunately, the ride there was now as comfortable as sitting on the couch.

When we arrived Pat got on his horse and led us down

the side road toward the big open pasture between *Pat's World* and the main *Center*. He had us do some exercises for emergency stops. We did this over and over again as we walked and trotted to the gate of the pasture.

This paddock is very big and long. It has tall grass beaten down where other riders have carved a trail. Off in the distance is a hill that you can't see over from the bottom. Once over the hill it more or less levels off all the way to a large car park.

Helen and I both knew how to ask our horses to canter so there was no need for instructions. Pat set us the following task: He says, "I am going to ride up the top of the hill and wait for you there. One at a time I want you to canter to me looking at my hat all the time. Do not take our eyes off my hat. It doesn't matter who goes first."

Pat left us at the gate and rode away. When he was far enough so he could not hear, Helen and I began our chatter about who should go first. I had butterflies big as houses so I made Helen go first. And, off she went. STEADY AS YOU PLEASE.

Now, it was my turn. I either get off and say, "No." or go. I went. For the first 200 metres this felt rough and I had a lot of fear response. I never took my eyes off Pat's hat even when he took it off to swat at something. I thought this might be why I was staying on. By 300 metres I had already gotten a feel for what Buddy was doing and my body fell into his rhythm. My body figured out where it had to be to feel like I was just rolling with the punches. The hill caused Buddy to lift his energy. They were big powerful strides and very different than they had been on the flatter ground. But because he was going up hill it felt like slow motion. Already I had gone longer than ever, and it was LONG ENOUGH to feel a change. It is amazing even to me how fast this change can happen. As I previously acknowledged, Pat is a masterful teacher.

We sat up on the hill with Pat and chatted non-stop. When we quieted down he said in that deep calm teacher's voice, "Now, I want you to walk back down to the gate and canter up and go past me. You can go as far as you would like. Just a little ways past or all the way if you want."

It was not any easier to start the second canter than it had been the first, but it took a lot less time to feel Buddy's rhythm and to be in harmony with it. When I approached Pat he asked me to count the number of fingers he was holding up. I did, he changed them and I counted again. I was really laughing by this time. I still knew I was cantering but I was cantering AND doing something else too! When I was very near he said take off your hat and put it back on. I did and as I did I wanted Buddy to go faster. I asked Buddy to go as fast as he could all the way to the parking lot. I was hoot'in and holler'in. The whole *Center* and everyone on the neighbouring mountains could hear me. When I turned around here was Helen cantering over the rise of the hill passing Pat with her hat in her hand.

We did this two more times. Each time Pat added some small task that seemed to make the act of cantering less and less the focus of what we were doing.

At the end of the session Pat gave us the task to canter up this pasture 4 times each morning for the next week. By the third day we were racing each other and talking to each other all the way to the top. The ride seemed less and less eventful. When we were cantering up the hill with arms outstretched like Kate Winslett on the bow with Leonardo Di Caprio in the film Titanic and I was talking to Buddy saying, "Go Buddy, Go". I knew I was ready to find the next edge of fear with cantering, because although this was fun, I had learned what there was to learn. I am not by any stretch a competitive person but I felt pride knowing that PacMan had never beaten Buddy up the hill even with a big head start. Oh, how things change.

Doing our assigned task. Riding up the hill 4 times each morning.

These three problems of not getting close enough, getting too close, and not staying long enough are why so many people take SO LONG to get where it is they are trying to go. Yes, there is a time for repetition and practise of what you can already do comfortably. That can cause your skills to improve. Here, however, we're talking about engaging in activities that you are likely avoiding altogether or where there is little or no progress.

I am a fast learner BECAUSE I understand how to directly transform fear by MOVING CLOSER, STAYING LONGER and I know how to not make these three now seemingly simple mistakes when I do.

Action

Stephanie Burns

CHAPTER 8

Don't Think, Just Do It

The bravery strategy of *MOVE CLOSER, STAY LONGER* is only going to be effective if you can get out there to use it. When it comes to taking action humans are notoriously good procrastinators. Because we are designed to avoid discomfort, pain and fear and because many normal activities related to goals are boring, frustrating, painful and frightening, our brain is constantly engaged in the process of figuring out how to keep us away from experiences that lead to these emotions. And, never more so than when fear awaits us. This was the significant finding while researching adult learners for my PhD.

Knowing what I had learned about motivation from my

University studies I felt it would be wholly unfair of me to leave you with a strategy for transforming your fear knowing that motivation to take action IS going to be a problem. I am able to get out there to take frequent and consistent actions BECAUSE I have a very good set of strategies to motivate myself to get off the couch. Some days it is just too cold, or Australia is playing cricket and the game is being aired on TV. I use these strategies ALL THE TIME. They are offered here because you too will need them.

One of the biggest lessons in managing your own behaviour is about the consequences of not knowing how to control what you think about.

Thinking about some tasks in advance causes your brain to "see" you engaged in the activity. If the activity you are imagining is likely to cause a negative emotional response then your brain, rightly and correctly, is going to present you with a good enough reason to avoid the task! It is trying to protect you.

If you can control what you allow yourself to think about, you will have a better chance of at least starting some challenging action because you will delay the onset of the fear response.

After a few days at the *Center* we were offered to bring our horses and tack to Pat and Linda's house where we were spending most of our down time. They have a paddock next to the house and tack on the veranda.

To ride to the house meant either going over a small drainage ditch, over logs, up a hill by the pond or taking the long way around. The first day I rode Buddy back to the house I got to the ditch and he jumped it. Well, golly gee did I have a FEAR NOW experience! But because I was happy to be on the other side, I did not give this any thought for the rest of the day.

Later in the day I found myself ruminating about the experience of Buddy's jump over the ditch. It is a very jolting experience if you do not know it is coming. I generated a good dose of ANTICIPATED FEAR about taking this route to the house again just by thinking about the past event.

It was interesting to observe my brain during this time. It imagined that going over the logs would be easier. THAT HAD NOT BEEN THE THOUGHT BEFORE. I overheard myself in my internal voice telling Helen and Pat and Linda good reasons why I kept going the long way around. I was rehearsing what to say just so that I did not have to confront my fear.

My experience with this kind of psychological behaviour allowed me to understand the dynamic at work here and to do something useful. I knew if I allowed it to continue my mind would figure out a way to never go over that ditch again. My brain tried to convince me of reasons why it might be better to keep Buddy over in the student's horse yards and travel over there several times a day.

I also knew a few other things. I was in no real danger, and I would likely have to take Buddy and Nugget over this kind of terrain a thousand times in the future so avoiding this was highly counterproductive to my long-term goal. Maybe one day there would not be a long way around and I would be really stuck.

DON'T THINK is an excellent strategy for those times when thinking in advance causes the fear response to begin and your brain starts figuring out how to protect you. I just DIDN'T THINK now about how I was going to get home next time.

By not thinking about the upcoming experience I gave myself a chance to get closer to the time and place where jumping the ditch or not jumping the ditch had to be decided. I could always choose to get off or go the long way if the fear response was too intense. In the meantime though, I was giving myself another chance to learn by not committing to avoidance so early plus I was saving myself all that travel between the house and the student's horse pens.

The next day once again the shortest path home was the path over the ditch. I rode up to it and stopped. Until that moment I did not allow myself to think about it. It was only in that moment I thought about it so I could make a decision. I did feel nervous being over my first edge of fear but I was nowhere near being over Edge #2. I hesitated only slightly and asked Buddy to go forward. I trusted Buddy to know what he had to do to get to the other side and trusted myself to not fall off.

I know there are going to be people who know the *Center* who are saying, WHAT DITCH is she talking about? All I can say is go look closely over by the small covered arena on the house side. If you bend down really low you will see that there IS a ditch there! It was a ditch to me!

If I had allowed my thinking to control my behaviour earlier I would not have had the opportunity to have this experience on this day. I would not have had less fear the next time.

An important point to be made is that in the end it is getting to the place where the opportunity exists to take action that is more important than what you do when you get there.

If I had gotten to that point and then decided to get off Buddy to walk it would not have been a bad result. I would have allowed myself to get as close as I could before making my decision. On another day getting to the ditch and choosing to go over it will be easier still. Someday it is quite likely ditches will not be an issue at all. I will also say, "What ditch?"

Remember that for the bravery strategy to be useful you have to be where it can be used. You have to give yourself the best possible chance to get as close as you can to the time and/or place of the frightening event. If you never get there you won't have any chance for change.

How do you "not think"?

I do know that once your brain gets on a negative track, turning it off is not easy. It is very hard to "not think". Your brain does what it does either because you are asking it to do that ("Do I feel like practicing riding down hills today?") or because you always allow it to do whatever it wants to do. It is YOUR brain, however, and you can control what it is allowed to think about.

One way you have of stopping your brain from going into thoughts that are not useful is to teach it to respond instantly to a few powerful commands. Your brain needs to learn that if you catch it thinking useless, fear provoking thoughts, you will insist that it respond to your commands of:

"Don't think about it."
"Don't go there!"
"Just do it"
"Just go."
"Get up now!"
"Get off it"

It is likely your brain will thumb its nose at you the first few times you do this. It will be thinking you cannot be serious. Remember you have most likely been asking your brain to decide what you will do and will not do based on its perceptions of what is going to be harmful to you for most of your life.

Your brain might well get a shock of disbelief when you tell it,

"No, I am deciding that we will keep moving toward this task!" If in the instant you catch your brain going into counterproductive thoughts that will lead to avoidance you tell it sternly and decisively "Don't go there!" It will respond and learn.

It is your brain and it is trying its best to serve you. When it learns that you seriously mean for it not to entertain certain thoughts at specific times it will bow to your leadership.

Stephanie Burns

CHAPTER 9

Do Think

Where Strategy #1 worked well for me was if I was coming up to something I had to do that was short and quick like jumping the ditch or riding to *Pat's World* the first time.

But it was not very effective at the times when I was sitting in the house and had a lot of choices about whether or not I was going to do something at all. And, of course, if I am not getting out there at all, I most certainly am not making any progress on changing, neutralising or learning to cope with the more frightening aspects of horsemanship in my world. In situations where I had a lot of choice and no real external pressure on me to act, Strategy #2, DO THINK was an excellent strategy to get myself motivated.

Where Strategy #1 said DON'T THINK, Strategy #2 says, DO THINK. You DO engage your brain. But you carefully CONTROL WHAT you allow your brain to think.

You have 2 options: Choose to think about positive results, or conversely even worse situations happening IN THE FUTURE if you DON'T TAKE ACTION NOW.

At about the middle of our stay Pat and Linda had to fly to Utah to deliver a 2 day *Success with Horses* event. They do these all over the world and it was Utah's turn. Helen and I were invited to go along. The plan was to head to the local Pagosa Springs airport on Friday and board a small-ish 11 seat private jet and arrive in Utah Friday night for a Saturday morning start. Of course, we said again, "Yes, yes, yes". This was on Monday. Friday was a long way off.

Monday night and Tuesday we expressed a lot of excitement about making the trip. By Wednesday my brain was starting to think not about the fun of the trip but the flight in the small-ish 11 seat private jet to get there.

I won't bore you again with my internal ruminations but know that they were bad and strong. DON'T THINK about it, JUST DO IT was not working because most of the really bad thoughts would wake me in the middle of the night. My brain is tricky that way. It does things in the middle of the night that it knows it can't get away with in the light of day.

By Thursday I was thinking more about being nervous the next day than I was focusing on what I was supposed to be doing. So, I sat under a tree and commanded my brain to think about staying at the *Center* for the weekend, ALL ALONE. My brain did not like thinking about this and kept flipping back to the plane ride. But I dragged it back kicking and screaming to my weekend being spent at the ranch alone. I vividly created the image of the house empty and no one to ride Buddy with. I created images of eating with other students in the dining hall and taking calls from Helen telling stories about where she, Pat, Linda and the other *Parelli* gang were eating.

The thought of not being there was now VERY DEPRESSING. With these internal experiences in place I could quickly draw on them any time my brain tripped over to the thoughts of flying. And, it worked. In this case thinking about HOW BAD I was going to feel did the trick. Sometimes it is better to think about how good you will feel. As an aside, it did take just a little bit of Strategy 1 GET OFF IT, JUST DO IT just before we got in the car to go to the airport. I had to do that several times until we were underway and the plane levelled off and my concern for the flight disappeared altogether.

All of your thoughts about the future get evaluated for emotional significance. This strategy ensures that you generate thoughts that are positive and motivating or negative and motivating. The rule goes something like this:

> ***If avoidance of an emotional experience,***
> ***hurts enough, or the pay off is big enough,***
> ***it will get done!***

Linda Parelli in her matching airplane outfit. On our way to Utah.

It is very important to know that how you imagine you will "feel" informs your decision about what you will do or not do. If you think about how you will "feel" giving a speech, or taking a test, and that thought brings to mind images AND those images lead to fear then you will do whatever it takes to avoid experiencing those feelings. How? Your brain will help you to NOT experience that bad feeling by avoiding the activity. It really is a double bind.

The game with DO THINK is choosing wisely the POINT in time that you focus on. Rather than focusing on the event itself, you focus on the future.

The goal is to think about a point in the future where you will either: Feel better for having done the task, or feel worse for not having done the task.

You may have been taught that THINKING POSITIVELY is the best motivation and recoil when you hear other people being negative. But please know that THINKING NEGATIVELY can be a much more motivating force, and most definitely so for some people.

A thought that leads to a consequence of embarrassment can easily override the consequence of being afraid for some. So, too, can thoughts that lead to other losses. For instance, the thought of having wasted a lot of time and money if I quit playing with horses now is very motivating. Let alone the thought of losing a good reason to hang out with Pat and Linda.

There were times when I cannot find a positive feeling or benefit in the future. In those cases I am not afraid to look for negative consequences. If it causes me to initiate even one more step toward my goal then it is a good strategy!

CHAPTER 10

Just Start, Decide Later

Although I use the first two strategies a lot there are times when they do not work for me. This is usually when the fear of doing something is just about starting it. I know that if I can start I will be fine. Some times, too, the kinds of negative thoughts I have are so ingrained that I cannot conjure up better or worse ones to replace them, or DON'T THINK, JUST DO IT just doesn't work. My thoughts keep running back to ones that created a strong ANTICIPATED FEAR response and it is beyond me to stop them no matter how commanding my GET OFF IT message is delivered to my brain.

I found this motivation strategy first out on the athletics

track. I named this strategy JUST START, DECIDE LATER.

When I am not doing research and writing reports or studying horsemanship I train as a sprinter. I can do as many as 11 or 12 activities related to this goal each week. Overall it is very challenging. You would not think there was anything frightening about sprinting, would you? Well, that's because you might have never had to sprint 400m.

I am a 100m sprinter but sometimes my training in the off-season requires that I do 400m sprints. Based upon my past experience of sprinting over 400m the protective systems in my brain absolutely scramble together to PROTECT me from completing (or even starting) a 400m session. I believe my brain really believes that I am going to die right there on the track. If I left it to my brain to make the decision about what I would do or not do it would most likely lead me to 1) change coaches; 2) quit; 3) hit my leg with a hammer so I had a good enough excuse to not start!

In this case there is no image positive enough or more negative than what I know will be my experience of sprinting 400m. And, DON'T THINK, JUST DO IT just doesn't get it! How I overcome my motivation to NOT run 400m is to modify DON'T THINK, JUST DO IT.

What I do is I commit to DON'T THINK, JUST START. In this case to sprint a hard 100m, and THEN decide if I want to keep running. If not, I will stop. What I know now from experience is that it is easier to keep doing what you are doing than it is to change it. After running those first 100m the last thing I want to do is stop at this stage! It is funny how a few seconds of movement in one direction causes me to change. It is HARDER to stop than it is to keep going.

On the days I am struggling to find motivation to get out

with my horse Nugget I commit to do 10 minutes in the direction of Nugget and if after 10 minutes I want to stop, I will. In 10 minutes I can get Nugget, warm up with a few games and saddle him. I usually have his full attention within the 10 minutes and I can see the curiosity question of, "What are we doing today?" on his face. Within 10 minutes he is most usually following me wherever I go with interest and enthusiasm.

I have the timer on my watch set for 10 minutes. When the alarm goes off I decide right then if I want to continue or stop. If at that time I don't want to do this session, I stop. I know that at least I got out there and tried. What is important to know is that I have never just stopped at that point. I find it is easier to keep going than to take the saddle off, put everything away and look at Nugget's face which is saying, "Hey, I thought we were going to play!"

The power of this strategy is being honest with yourself that you are truly only committing to start, and that after 10 minutes you can stop if you do not want to continue.

I think you will be surprised at how much impact 10 minutes of action in the direction of the task can be on your motivation and the number of steps you can take toward changing a fear response to an activity.

This is also a useful strategy if you have a particular part of a task that causes fear and is causing you to avoid the task altogether. For instance, in the early days on I found that my concern for trotting caused me to avoid getting on Nugget altogether. And, I really needed to have a lot of experience getting on even if it was just to sit on him or go for walks. I used JUST START, DECIDE LATER to not let my ever present concern for trotting stop me from doing other aspects of riding that I would benefit from doing.

I would do 10 minutes in which I would sit on Nugget for five minutes while he stood still, and then ride him at the walk in the arena for 5 more minutes. Then, and only then, would I decide if trotting would be in the cards for that session. Some days I was so bored walking that I could not wait to trot for short spells, on other days the fear edge was too close to choose trotting as a step. The point is I was not letting the fear of trotting get in the way of me at least getting out there and being on Nugget. And as I did more sitting and walking I did get more confident. I did on some days choose to trot. Eventually those experiences diminished my fear of trotting to not even a blip on the fear radar.

This strategy works for lots of things not just activities you fear. If you've been procrastinating about any task, even mundane ones like cleaning the windows, set a timer and play the game: How much can I do in 10 minutes? Then do as much as you can. At the end of 10 minutes you can stop, but I bet you that in most, if not all cases, it will feel better now to continue. Use this strategy to clean up your life.

CHAPTER 11

Measure and Count

Every action you take, no matter how small is one more step taken toward your goal that you do not ever have to take again. Every action has an impact on getting you where it is you are trying to go. In the pursuit of goals we sometimes begin to think that if we cannot do a lot it isn't worth doing. That thinking is a fast path to quitting because in a long goal pursuit there are going to be times when other circumstances dictate that time for your goal is scarce.

Counting is good. Every minute, every inch, every well-crafted sentence counts. Counting is good for two things. One thing it is good for is to measure change. The other is to motivate yourself to do more than you otherwise would.

We arrived home from America in early September with the experiences from our time at the *Pat Parelli Center* firmly in tow. Nugget and Decker arrived home a few days later from the Gwinn's farm in Braidwood. I had now been away for over 10 weeks and my work was backlogged over the top of my desk. It didn't matter that I was motivated to spend time with Nugget, it was just not appropriate to abandon my work to be with him. Rather than seeing this as wasted time I did what I could do.

I had to take time out to feed him so I took a few extra minutes at that time to groom him and play MOVE CLOSER, STAY LONGER around his hindquarters. Every inch counted. It was one less inch I would have to deal with later. When it was time to bring him to his overnight yard (our paddocks were devastated from the drought and turning to dust) I didn't just walk him in. I played some of the *Parelli 7* Games with him. I backed him or side-passed him all the way from the paddock and then backed him through his gate or did some other creative task.

You can always do SOMETHING even with very limited time. The motivation to do so is the knowledge that every little thing counts. Counting in minutes and inches made me always think to do something.

Counting is also a way to measure change. It is very easy to forget that changes ARE happening every time we take useful action. By setting a goal to count to a specific number of instances or get closer by a certain number of metres allows time to pass before expecting a change to occur, or quitting because one is not happening fast enough. Some things just take a long time and we can be very blind to progress unless it is measured in small units.

I motivate myself by paying attention to:
How many more?
How much longer?
How much further?

Nugget and I were in the middle of the Level 2 program when I got home. We were ready to start what are called *THE IMPULSION PROGRAMS*. These are riding patterns that help horses balance between what is called their GO and WHOA. For horses who do not like to stop or who like to get faster and faster when ridden these patterns help change that. Horses who just don't want to go change in the other direction. Nugget had a good go and whoa but he is a horse that is curious about everything. His problem (or my problem) is that Nugget has the attention span of a gnat. He's like a child with ATTENTION DEFICIT DISORDER who has just downed a jug of red cordial. The impulsion programs were going to be good for him.

You are meant to do each program, there are 8 in all, for 7 days in a row before moving on to the next. You are then to revisit the previous programs every so often.

Nugget and I started with a program called *POINT TO POINT*. I went about setting up 2 orange cones at the opposite ends of the arena. By the time I set up the second one Nugget had trotted over to the first. He had it in his teeth. He was rearing while he flipped it up and down smacking it on his nose. That's Nugget and why I thought these programs would be good for him. I walked back and retrieved my horse and repositioned the cone. I then got on and positioned Nugget just in front of the first cone.

The program was to ride in a straight line between the cones without having to correct his direction. You are meant to do this first at a walk, then a trot, and eventually a canter. I asked for a walk and the first step took us to the right. I lifted the rein and put him back in line with the cone on the other side of the arena. Then we went left. Then he saw a bird and went right, then left, then a ball and continued left some more. Between the 2 cones 34 metres apart I made 23 corrections. It was going to be a LONG AND WINDING ROAD.

Once we got there we stopped facing the cone. Since this was clearly hard for him I gave him a good minute to think about it. I then backed him away from the cone and turned him 180 degrees so he faced the other cone. I sat there for another minute and then asked for a walk. Left, right, left, right. 18 corrections. By the end of my first day on this program in which Nugget and I did 20 repetitions I knew the starting point. When asked to go in a straight line for 34 metres we need 12 corrections.

The next day we played for awhile and then set up the cones. I positioned Nugget at the first and asked for a walk. 21 corrections. The second go, 11 corrections. By the end of this session we had made it between the cones 3 times with less than 10 corrections each time.

On the fifth day Nugget walked briskly and confidently from cone to cone with no corrections so we graduated to trotting. I face the other cone and ask for a trot. He trots five or six strides and does a big 180 degree arc and stops in front of the cone we just left. He has excited energy I could feel him asking, "Is this right? Is this right?!" I stroked his neck and said, "Nice try." Turned him around and trotted him off. This time he bobbed and weaved to the cone at the far end of the arena.

It was 8 days before we were ready to canter. When I asked he cantered. STRAIGHT TO THE GATE!

Now, if you are getting bored reading this story, spare a thought for me. I had to live through it. I know a hundred people who could not get through the impulsion programs because ALL they focus on in life are the big changes, getting the big result fast. In this situation their focus would be on what they were not doing yet, on NOT GETTING IT. I survived as a student because I supported my perceptions by counting and measuring the changes each day. I knew he was getting better at this task in every session. He was getting more confident too. I could have easily left sessions in total frustration and given up on the impulsion programs. Instead I left excited enough to record these changes and to look forward to the next days session.

When time and circumstance or looking for big changes affects your motivation then remember to take actions just for the sake of counting or measuring. How many seconds or minutes can you do something today? Go find out. Then, what can you do to add seconds or minutes over the next few weeks. Make that be THE goal. Find out how close in centimetres or metres you can get to the object of fear today. Then, do whatever it takes to get closer still. After a week go and measure again.

Learn to look for positive changes in how long, how close or how many and celebrate every time a change occurs. Trust that a little movement over a long period of time is the best path to achieving significant goals when fear is involved.

Stephanie Burns

CHAPTER 12

Challenge Your Assumptions With Quality Information

As humans we are notorious for making things up for which we have no evidence or experience. I had a long list of fears about horses and riding long before Nugget ever arrived. Some of these were installed by well meaning cautious other people, but many of these had no basis whatsoever and turned out to be quite irrational. Left unchecked who would have blamed me if I never took even one step toward achieving a horsemanship goal.

I admit that I make up all kinds of stories about people, places, objects, situations and tasks that I believe I will be afraid of even though I have NO experience and NO knowledge to base those beliefs upon. I notice that I tell these stories to myself over and over again and scare myself silly.

The trouble with doing this is that my motivation and behaviour is affected negatively long before I give myself a chance for learning and having experiences that will have a counterbalancing effect.

We were invited by Kate and Owen Gwinn to come to their ranch in Braidwood for a few days. This would give us a chance to enjoy a few good meals with friends and tell them the stories of our adventures with Pat and Linda. At this point we were very committed to seeking opportunities to expand our horsemanship bubble and there is only so much we can do at our place. We packed up a few clothes, our horses and headed out for some time OFF THE ARENA.

Kate and Owen have a cattle ranch for which horses are fun and a means to carry out their work. On the first two days Helen and I played with our horses in their big arena and round yard and had fun being in bigger spaces.

All around us were cattle. There were bulls in some pens and cows with calves in others. There were pregnant cows and just plain ole steers cows being readied for market. I KNEW NOTHING about cattle. Everything I did know I MADE UP. If you'd have asked me to go for a ride out in a big pasture with a bunch of cows I would not have had any way to know if that was a good thing to do or a bad thing to do.

On the morning of our last day there was a job that had to be done. The heifers in the house paddock that had delivered their calves needed to be separated from those yet to give birth. I had to ask what a HEIFER was (I am still not certain I am spelling it correctly!) and found out that these are cows that are just now having their first calf. I don't know what you call a cow when they are having their second calf.

We were invited to go along. Then, the real questions started. We wanted to know EVERYTHING about being around cows and about horses being around cows and about danger being near cows. At last we asked, "Do you think this is something we can do?" We were assured, with as much confidence as realistically can be given when you are doing something with a horse, that it was. Nugget had been ridden by Owen for cattle work at Braidwood while we were away and Decker was just well, Decker. She was confident in all the situations we had been in to date.

Ask other people for an interpretation

Horses are a bit tricky in this regard because they CAN absolutely be dangerous given the wrong horse, or the right horse in the wrong situation. They are big, strong, heavy prey animals.

Regardless of your goal it is very important to test your assumptions about people, places, objects, situations and tasks that cause you to have an ANTICIPATED FEAR response. In many instances information is all that is needed to assuage the fear and motivate action. Lack of accurate information can affect your ability to sustain action or repeat an action in the future.

Humans in general don't deal well with unfamiliar things and uncertain situations. When we find ourselves in these situations our brain goes to work to create a meaning for the experience. If you have already predisposed yourself to interpret things that are bad, then your brain is going to be more apt to look in the HOW IS THIS BAD FOR MY HUMAN box for its first interpretation.

Having a friend who can answer questions from THEIR experience is important. Your goal is to gather information that allows you to say, "This is what I might see, might feel and what that means."

Remember, too, that in many cases what you are trying to achieve is not to "like" or "enjoy" the sensation but to have no reaction to it at all. Accurate information can be the fastest path to getting over niggling fears.

Watching how other people respond to the same situation

Some things are better learned not by asking but by observing. The next morning we had breakfast and asked more questions after which we all got our horses and saddled up. We played with them on the ground to see if the side they woke up on today was a good side. We then got on and played some more. I watched closely what Kate and Owen did to get ready. They did everything we were taught to do and even though this was a job for them every care was taken in their PRE-RIDE checks. Everything was good. The four of us rode out into the big house pasture.

I tucked Nugget in behind Kate and Owen. This was unfamiliar territory for me and watching what they did at each new place helped me know what to expect when I got there. A little hill to go down here, a crop of rocks there, tall grass here and so on.

Kate thought she knew where the cows were hanging out and I was just amazed that you could have a big enough place that you had to think about where a whole bunch of cows might be. And this was just one paddock! Sure enough after a ride of 5 or so minutes we found the cattle scattered on the other side of the dam. The job was to move all the cattle toward a closed gate, then find the cattle that had calves and drive them to an open gate further up the fence and into another paddock. That would leave the cows yet to give birth in the house paddock where they could be watched.

WELL! There were SO many things that I didn't know, I didn't even want to start to ask questions. I watched what Kate and Owen did and listened to the information they thought we should have. I learned about the zones of a cow and the herd and the pressure needed to cause it to move one way or the other. I learned that it is not always apparent which calf belongs to which mother and this is important because a cow will NOT care for a calf that isn't its own. And the calves, they don't seem to HAVE A CLUE.

I watched how Kate and Owen decided who belonged to who and how they went about walking into the herd without disturbing it and caused the cows they didn't want to move away and the mother and calf they did want move out of the herd and up the fence line. Every time one or more pairs were separated they were slowly driven up the fence line and shown the gate.

Then a mother and calf were pointed out and it was our turn. I hadn't changed much so I asked Helen to go first. She moved Decker toward the herd but as she got closer she seemed to have trouble controlling Decker's direction and forward movement. Decker was showing signs of lacking confidence with the cattle. Helen was a good *Parelli* student. She dropped the intention of separating the cow and calf and instead helped Decker gain more confidence by approaching and retreating until Decker could get into the mix of it. With that success she backed Decker out and allowed her to have some time to soak on the experience. Well done!

It was my turn and Nugget had no trouble wanting to be with the cows. They were a curiosity to him, oh yeah PLAYMATES! I was amazed how easily he followed my focus on Mum and the little one we were seeking. I put my eyes on the cow's hindquarters and he went right there. He followed that cow intensely. All the other cows KNEW it wasn't them he was after and moved out of the way. In no time he had worked the cow and calf out of the herd and up the fence line. I felt like I DIED AND WENT TO HEAVEN ON A HORSE.

This was simply fantastic. Going home to my desk and computer was not easy after this experience.

Your fears might simply be caused by not understanding what is normal or not normal. You might not be the best source of information about whatever it is you want to do. If that is the case find someone who is.

I feel a need here to add my first caveat. I must warn that all things are not equal in the world of information. I was very fortunate to have been brought toward horses and horsemanship by some of the most talented and knowledgeable people in the world. It is the same with my sprint training, I have had the benefit of being coached by a well-respected Olympic sprint coach. But I might not have been so lucky, and you might not have these same quality sources in your own goal pursuit. You want to choose wisely those that you listen to and who you believe to be well informed and who is not.

Who can you trust? How I personally judge the quality of a person's information is always by looking at the tangible evidence. Do they themselves do what they are suggesting I do, and if so, what is the result? For instance, if someone is giving me dietary advice for Nugget I want to see that person is following this same advice and that it is producing the good health in the horses they own. If they don't I will go somewhere else without hesitation!

Asking and observing are cheap and effective ways to fill in the gaps and keep you emotionally safe from MOVING TOO CLOSE TOO SOON.

CHAPTER 13

Use the Power of Commitments to Other People as Motivation

Have you noticed that it is much harder to avoid or cancel something if you have made plans to do it with someone else? This is because the discomforting emotion of guilt is often stronger than the fear or concern that would otherwise cause us to avoid taking that action if we were doing it alone.

This strategy came in handy on more than a number of occasions during my studies. I had Pat and Linda and dozens of *Parelli* instructors and students and many thousands of my own students watching what I was up to. When my motivation needed a little extra power I drew on this.

I now make plans to visit Kate and Owen every 6 weeks or

so. The quantum leaps in my horsemanship while I am there cannot be achieved at home. I can kick and scream in the days leading up to a trip about HOW WILL I GET MY WORK DONE but I DON'T THINK ABOUT IT and then DON'T THINK, DECIDE LATER such as in the car when I am a long way out of Sydney and approaching the gates to their ranch.

Being in a class can heighten our motivation to move closer and stay longer. Note that I am now happy to ride Buddy with other classmates.

I also make commitments to spend time with Pat and Linda. I invited them to stay with me on their most recent visit and that offered me another powerful lesson that expanded how I was using my own small place. On Friday of this week I will board another plane to America. This time I am going to Florida where I will spend a month with Pat and Linda at the winter *Pat Parelli Center*. Buddy will be waiting for me when I arrive.

Think about how obligations and commitments to others might affect your motivation. Then, make some plans. Your brain might throw a FIT leading up to it but that's okay, that's its job. You'll find it much easier to act than avoid.

CHAPTER 14

Do Lots of What You Can Do and a Little of What You are Afraid of

When your fears are overwhelming your ability to use *MOVE CLOSER, STAY LONGER*, your number one priority should be to STAY IN THE GAME NO MATTER WHAT.

By becoming consumed with thoughts about what we cannot or are not doing because of fear, we support ourselves avoiding more and more action. The longer you delay taking action the harder it is going to be to get going again.

When I would get into periods where my fear of riding was very high I found that the fear also got in the way of me spending time playing with Nugget on the ground. That meant there was no progress at all and not much chance that I was going to find the opportunity to once again move closer to riding.

In these situations I encourage myself to get out there and do what I can do, and in the midst of that I commit to do just a few minutes working on the activity causing fear. There were many days I took the saddle to the arena and left it on the side. I would play with Nugget on the ground and not think about whether I was going to ride until later. In many cases the ground session was so good and so much fun that I was compelled to saddle Nugget. In some of those cases I got on and had a ride. If I did not get out there to do a lot of what I could do confidently, these opportunities to work on the stuff that was causing fear wouldn't have been done. That fear would have stopped all action and all opportunity for future action.

You do not always have to be working on the scary stuff. Life is long and so too are significant goal pursuits. Let things evolve and know that the only path to failing to achieve the goal is to quit taking action altogether.

Some people questioned why I put Nugget in a yard at night instead of leaving him in the paddock. I understand that Nugget would love to be grazing in the paddock overnight but I also know that when he was new to my life there was very little I was comfortable doing. I could imagine that on a bad day, or during a bad patch when lots of fear events emerged, I would happily just chuck him some hay, say, "Hello" over the fence and be done with it. I could imagine there might be days I would then not have touched him at all. I knew this would be a fast path to never touching him again.

The reason I choose to have Nugget in an overnight yard is to support myself having contact with him, moving him, making physical contact with him and playing with him at least twice each day. It might not have been much but I was staying in the game. At times this support strategy was how I passed time waiting to be resilient enough to MOVE CLOSER again, to get out there to play with or ride him in a more formal session. Had I not supported myself by doing a lot of what I could do (eg catch, halter, walk with, feed, watch, rub etc) I might have abandoned the goal due to lack of action before I got to Level 1.

So, what can you do comfortably in relation to your goal? Maybe simply watching is all you can do. If so, get out there and do that. Give yourself a chance to find the resilience to apply the bravery strategies again, one more time, to take one more step.

After becoming comfortable cantering up the big hill, Helen and I often took ourselves to the BIG TOP to finish a session where we would have to canter around corners. We did a lot of what we could do for confidence and experience and a little bit of what scared us everyday.

CHAPTER 15

Time Will Pass

I have always found motivation in the thought that time is going to pass whether I do anything or not. I know that I am going to wake up in the future being able to do something I want to do or NOT. It is that simple. That thought compels action more than any other. I will be a very cranky old woman if at the end of my life I have to reconcile that I didn't end up the places I wanted to go because I was unable to motivate small consistent steps.

Nearly a year has passed since I wrote the Foreword to this book. More than 300 days of opportunity to take action have passed.

Interestingly, fear has not played much of a part in my horsemanship goals over this time. But that is not to say that I have not faced new challenges that could have generated fear. I have discovered that with frequent use and application the Bravery Strategy of Move Closer Stay Longer has transformed my approach to learning. Where it was initially the method of taking actions that transformed fear, it has become a WAY of approaching each new challenge that interrupts anticipated fear!

Let me explain with a story.

In January 2004, I visited with Pat and Linda again, this time at the *Parelli Center* in Florida. I was there to teach at the annual *Parelli* Professionals Conference and of course, a bit of horseplay and riding tossed in. During my time there I noticed that I was highly inspired and moved every time I saw someone riding bareback. It was somehow quite beautiful to me.

In the past this would have caused me to sit on the couch and daydream about doing this myself. You know now what that would have caused!

Anticipated Fear!

And, I do not need to rewrite the lessons of this book here for you to know what that would have set up for me as a learner – let's just say lots of learning and motivation blocks.

But I didn't do that!

I did not think about ME riding bareback. I only thought about OTHER people riding bareback.

What I did think about was where I could go in relation to that challenge and feel a little something.

I started to stand on a box while playing with Nugget so I would be up above him. We played all of the games and did this until it felt wonderful to have him standing near me where I could look down on his head and back. I groomed him from up there too. I would brush his mane and back. And sometimes I would lean on his back with one hand while I reached to brush a far away spot.

I loved this time. Within a couple of days I was laying over his back, giving him a good rub. On the fourth day, I swung my leg over his back and lay there with my head on the side of his neck. I stayed there a long time. I got off and I got on and I got off and I got on until this felt like the best place to be.

I sat on Nugget for a long time for a couple of days until I just felt like asking him to walk a ways. The feel was amazing. I did this over and over again. I never got tired of being with him in this way and I looked forward to it more than nearly anything else.

A few more days passed and I felt a little something in my stomach about asking for the trot, but the idea to ask for just a few steps was not too uncomfortable. So, I did. This was surprisingly easy and I felt no sense of imbalance. I asked again and again and again. By the next day I was out of the round yard and onto the arena. I had to just remember that it was important to give Nugget a bit of rest! I was so absorbed in my own fun with this it was easy to forget.

In the past I would have THOUGHT about the challenge of riding Nugget bareback. That thought would have set in motion ANTICIPATED FEAR and all of its consequences. I would have then had to use the Bravery strategy to take steps toward that challenge. I would have been feeling a lot along the way and I would be at risk of avoiding, procrastinating and perhaps even quitting.

Here I was inspired by images of other people riding bareback. But I did NOT think about riding bareback myself. I did not stimulate the fear. Instead, I used the same Move Closer Stay Longer strategy in my sessions with Nugget. Moving me closer to mount, to sit and to ride bareback.

The point of the story is this.

> ***IF you control what you think***
> ***which in turn affects the emotions generated***
> ***THEN***
> ***the Bravery Strategy can be used as a***
> ***Learning strategy to progress with your goal.***

I have had a wonderful time with Nugget over this past year.

I am back in Pagosa Springs with Linda and Pat now. It is July 2004. I have been reunited with Buddy and I wonder what adventures we will have while I am here. I watch other students and some things are inspiring me. I am not thinking about what I might or might not do myself. I am just enjoying the images of other people and the emotions that come with those images. At the same time I go to some place with Buddy everyday where I feel a little something. Not so much as to cause me to quit, but not so little that I am not learning.

Nugget and I preparing for my first bareback riding experience. Life is very good indeed.

I wish for you to go where it is you wish to be.

Acknowledgements

Writing this book turned out to be far more challenging than I had anticipated. Under normal circumstances I would have been teaching these concepts and learning how to tell my stories to bring those concepts to life to my students. I started an extended break from teaching in 2001 and that left me with no real opportunity for this material to naturally shape itself. When it came to writing this book I was dependent upon talking to myself, and the few people involved with the actual events.

This book would NOT exist if it were not for Linda and Pat Parelli, Helen and my equine partners, Nugget and Buddy. You all offered partnership, love, intelligence and humour that sustained me during the times I questioned just WHAT IN THE WORLD WAS THIS ALL ABOUT? You will discover the true nature of your contributions when you read this book. Helen, you will have to read this book to Nugget. He still has trouble turning the pages.

I would like to acknowledge my appreciation for past *Parelli* instructors Mark and Debbie for allowing me to just POP OVER as often needed to answer the first one million questions I had about horses and for letting me play with Cooper. Ken and Kathy for being available at all hours for phone calls when Nugget was still more a confusion to me than a partner.

I would especially like to thank Kate and Owen and Amy who are always at the ready to help Nugget learn at those times when he is just TOO MUCH HORSE for me to teach. For helping me to be a better human for my horses I am indebted. Our new friendship has much life in it.

I would not have been able to write a book on the topic of fear in the context of learning and achievement if it were not for Prof. Kym Adey of the University of South Australia who ensured that the opportunity to do a PhD program was possible. Your calm leadership sustained my belief that I COULD complete a PhD when I was very wobbly. I can still hear your voice. Dr. Bruce Johnson who fought a hard fight for me with my examiners, and my other supervisors, thank you. I simply would not possess the knowledge found on the pages of this book had you not helped me recognise that achieving a goal IS at times more important than the journey.

Lastly, thank you to the staff and instructors at the *Pat Parelli Center* in Pagosa Springs, Colorado. Neil Pye and Sue Shoemark, thanks for choosing Budman and PacMan. Those two confident horses enabled us to take full advantage of the opportunities the Center offered. Vonni Wilcox, you were THERE for me during the first *Parelli* project while I was building the *Parelli* support website. I needed you and you responded. I look forward to the working with you on our next projects in 2004.

Thanks Kalley for your gentle and competent care of Buddy and PacMan and always seeing they were where we needed them. Thank you to the staff of the ISC in Pagosa Springs for your good care of me. Coco, your photos are amazing, if I had known I looked that good on a horse I would have been less self-conscious.

Stephanie Burns

Made in the USA
Lexington, KY
20 November 2014